W9-DGN-064

GROWING AND LEARNING

The Playful Baby

130+ Quick Brain Boosting Activities for Infancy to 18 Months

By
Becky Daniel

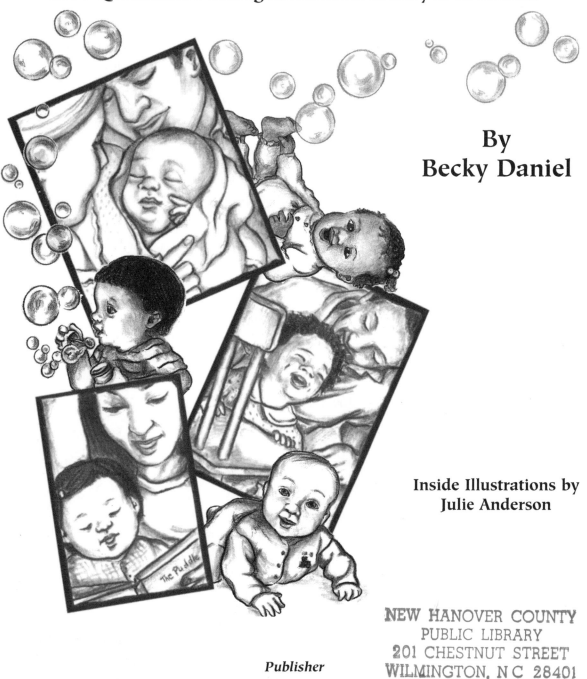

Inside Illustrations by
Julie Anderson

NEW HANOVER COUNTY
PUBLIC LIBRARY
201 CHESTNUT STREET
WILMINGTON, N C 28401

Publisher
Instructional Fair • T.S. Denison
Grand Rapids, Michigan 49544

Instructional Fair • TS Denison

All rights reserved. No part of this publication may be reproduced, stored in a retrieval system, or transmitted in any form or by any means, electronic, mechanical, photocopy, recording, or otherwise, without the prior written permission of the publisher. For information regarding permission write to: Instructional Fair • TS Denison, P.O. Box 1650, Grand Rapids, MI 49501.

About the Author ....

Becky Daniel is a parent, teacher, author, and editor—four distinctive yet interrelated professions. After graduating from California University at Long Beach, she taught kindergarten through eighth grade. When she began her family, she left the classroom to care for her first daughter and to pursue a career in writing at home.

Now the mother of three children—Amy, Sarah, and Eric—she edits a magazine and writes educational books from her home in Orcutt, California. Over the past 25 years she has written over 200 educational resource books.

She is also the author of a picture book, *Prince Poloka of Uli Loko,* a Hawaiian story for children, and *I Love You Baby,* a parenting book. In 1989 she was honored to have her biographical sketch and a list of her earlier works featured in Volume 56 of *Something About the Author.*

Credits ....

Author	Becky Daniel
Inside Illustrations	Julie Anderson
Project Director	Debra Olson Pressnall
Editors	Debra Olson Pressnall & Karen Seberg
Cover Art Direction/Design	Terri Moll
Graphic Layout & Icon Illustrations	Mark Conrad
Cover Photograph	© EyeWire

ISBN:1-56822-953-4
Growing and Learning: The Playful Baby
©2000 Instructional Fair • TS Denison
A Division of Instructional Fair Group, Inc.
A Tribune Education Company
3195 Wilson Drive NW, Grand Rapids, MI 49544

All Rights Reserved • Printed in USA

Dear Parents,

This is an exciting time for you and your baby. It is also a crucial time in your child's education. If you are like most parents, you may have a feeling that something is being left undone, unsaid, incomplete. Do you feel that you would like to get a head start in providing appropriate activities for your child's intellectual, motor, and emotional development? Then this is the book for you! *Playful Baby* is designed to help you understand the basic learning patterns of babies and give you simple games and activities to enrich your baby's learning.

In the first months, you will notice that your baby's organized patterns are his/her reflexes—breathing, swallowing, rooting, sucking, crying, and grasping. Soon other reflexes will become apparent—smiling, gazing, and shutting out stimuli. In the months to come, other behavior patterns will develop—moving at will, communicating needs, and expressing delight. By the time your baby is one year old, his/her abilities will include manipulating things and playing purposefully with toys.

The simple games and activities in this book are specially designed to help you build on what your baby can already do at each stage of development and will enrich his/her intellectual growth. Do you know you can use music to teach your infant coordination, or a silk scarf to teach blocking out stimuli, or a rattle to teach grasping? The secret to success does not lie in the games, equipment, or technique—it lies in your involvement. The fact that you are there, touching, cooing, and modeling learning, will make your play with your baby educational. As a bonus, as you role model learning, your child will not only master what you are teaching, he/she will realize that acquiring knowledge is exciting and fun. With the games herein, you can set a pattern of learning for your child that will last a lifetime. Celebrate learning, and your child will, too.

Today, you have the power to hold up a positive mirror to your baby—one that will reflect love and caring. Your touch and attention will teach your child the most important thing of all: he/she is loved.

Sincerely,

Becky Daniel

TABLE OF CONTENTS

INTRODUCTION

The Value of Play 6

PLAYING WITH YOUR NEWBORN TO TWELVE-MONTH-OLD

The Beginning– Playing with Your Newborn

Contemplate/Milestones 8
General Tips 9
Cry Language 10
Relaxed Breathing 11
Language of Love 12
Time to Eat 13
Flash the Light 14
Peekaboo 15
Squeeze Me 16
Bicycle Pedaling 17
Crawl and Swim 18
Sleeping 19
Being Awake 20
Smiling 21
Teaching Trust 22
Keeping Track 23

Little Changes– Playing with Your One-Month-Old

Contemplate/Milestones 24
General Tips 25
Rock-a-Bye, Baby 26
It's a Comfort 27
What's All the Fuss? 28
Let's Dance 29
Smile, Baby, Smile! 30
Hello, Baby 31
Goo, Goo, Gaga 32
Watch My Hands 33
Follow the Ball 34
Tinker Bell Socks 35
Shake and Rattle 36
Look There! 37
Fling Your Foot 38
Keeping Track 39

Big Changes– Playing with Your Two- to Three-Month-Old

Contemplate/Milestones 40
General Tips 41
Rattle, Rattle 42
Clap Your Hands 43
Babble, Babble 44

Up We Go! 45
Mirror, Mirror 46
Sniff, Sniff 47
Shhh, Listen 48
Making Faces 49
I See a Smile 50
Watch the Birdie 51
Busy Beeline 52
Bat the Ball 53
Jingle Bell Mobile 54
Keeping Track 55

Sit Up and Roll Over– Playing with Your Four- to Eight-Month-Old

Contemplate/Milestones 56
General Tips 57
Roly-Poly Bug 58
Over We Go 59
Up and Down 60
Here Sits Baby 61
Up We Go 62
Feelies 63
Looking at Books 64
Yoo Hoo! 65
That's My Name 66
Do You Know "No"? 67
Abracadabra 68
Buzz and Hum 69
Sleeping Turtle 70
Keeping Track 71

Creepy Crawly– Playing with Your Nine- to Twelve-Month-Old

Contemplate/Milestones 72
General Tips 73
Come and Get It 74
Pick Up 75
Busy Box 76
Choo Choo Train 77
Dance with Me 78
Cymbals 79
Poke 'n' Poke 80
I'm Proud of You 81
Play Day 82
Apple Pie, Pudding, and Pancakes 83
This Is the Way We Eat Our Food 84
Beanbag Drop 85
Arms Up! 86
Bo-Beep Play 87
Keeping Track 88

© Instructional Fair • TS Denison

PLAYING WITH YOUR TWELVE- TO EIGHTEEN-MONTH-OLD

Look at Me!
Fine Motor Development

Contemplate/Milestones 90
General Tips 91
Nice 92
Lights On, Lights Off 93
Filling Station 94
Take This One, Too 95
Blocks 96
Please Put It Back 97
Knock It Off! 98
Sorting Cereals 99
Go Fish 100
Turn the Page, Please 101
Play My Face 102
Paper Wads 103
Toss 104
Catch 105
Treasure Box 106
Keeping Track 107

All By Myself
Gross Motor Development

Contemplate/Milestones 108
General Tips..109
Boing 110
Peekaboo Box 111
Superman 112
London Bridge 113
Up, Up, and Away! 114
Going Down 115
Ring-Around the Rosy....................................116
Gotcha! 117
Rock-a-Bye, Baby..118
Drop the Hankie 119
Walk the Baby 120
Flying Baby 121
Hold On Tight 122
Toss It...123
Jump!..124
Keeping Track 125

"Dada, Mama"
Language Development

Contemplate/Milestones 126
General Tips..127
Shhhh...128
This Little Cow 129
Three Bears in the Bed 130
Ooooooh 131
Babble Back at Baby.....................................132

Name It!..133
Eye Winker 134
Match Up 135
Old MacDonald Had a Farm..........................136
Heeeere's Baby..137
"Mama or Dada?"..138
"Bye-Bye"...139
"Thank You" 140
"All Gone" 141
Time to Talk 142
Keeping Track 143

Copy Cat
Cognitive Development

Contemplate/Milestones 144
General Tips..145
How Do You Do? 146
Building Bridges 147
Does It Fit?..148
Go-Seek 149
Go-Hide 150
Look Up 151
Doodle, Doodle...152
Excuuuuse Me!..153
Good for You! 154
By Yourself 155
Here I Am 156
Push, Pull, Lift 157
Pick One, Any One 158
Bubbles! 159
Sniff, Sniff 160
Keeping Track 161

Mine!
Social/Emotional Development

Contemplate/Milestones 162
General Tips..163
Ping-Pong Pitch 164
Soothing Baby 165
Bear Wrestling 166
Good Night, Bear 167
Butterfly Flittering 168
Take a Bow...169
Playmates..170
Lights Out! 171
Peekaboo, Baby!...172
Where Does This Go?....................................173
We Love You 174
Look at Me!...175
Keeping Track 176

VALUE OF PLAY

Every baby is distinctly different from every other baby—even identical twins are unique from each other. But one thing all children have in common is their need to play. There is a powerful force within every human being which strives continuously for complete self-actualization. Parents may not notice this force in their infants, but as soon as babies begin to walk, this mysterious force causes them to begin demonstrating independence and self-direction. What is often misinterpreted as "defiant behavior" is actually a manifestation of a toddler's divine will to become an individual. Play is the place where a baby can bring about this dynamic life force and develop on every level: intellectually, physically, emotionally, socially, and creatively.

When a child is born, he has over a hundred billion brain cells. Through play, trillions of synapses develop connecting these hundred billion cells in the brain. Each time a baby is rocked, held, read to, and interacted with, new synapses develop and the baby's intellect is enhanced. Babies who are left unattended, not rocked and held or interacted with, can actually suffer brain damage. Play, although it sounds simple, must be taken seriously. Play is your child's work!

Physically, a child develops well-balanced, fine and gross motor skills during recreation. Toys are not just for fun. It is no accident that down through history, in all cultures, toys are a part of early childhood. Games with equipment teach the learner how to manipulate and, like the old adage says, "Practice makes perfect." Mother Goose rhymes, musical games, and dancing about is play with rhythm and rhyme that orchestrates balance, coordination, and grace. Before your child learns to walk, you can hold her and dance, prance, march, and move to music. She will experience the movements through her physical contact with you.

Emotionally, play is therapeutic. Since play is a natural medium for self-expression, it provides the baby with a safe space to experience, express, and celebrate feelings. In play, the toddler is given the opportunity to "play" out his accumulated feelings of tension, frustration, insecurity, aggression, fear, bewilderment, confusion. The more difficult and less obvious advantage of play is that it allows the child a place to learn how to handle anger and aggression. Although this is a long process, expressing turmoil openly in socially acceptable ways is vital for a child's emotional well-being. As a bonus, through play, children develop a sense of humor and an ability to show empathy to others. Emotionally speaking, play is vital to mental health and stability.

Creativity is a tremendous gift human beings are born with. Unfortunately, instead of being nurtured, often imaginations are stifled. As parents and teachers of young children, we must remember: in fantasy play, children are given a stage on which they can spotlight their creative nature. Children imagine whole scenarios and assimilate their learning through fanciful make–believe. Symbolic play, in which toys and dolls are used, allows toddlers an opportunity to practice every possible social situation. This exploratory play and experience with others is a prerequisite for the child to accomplish a positive self-image. And last but not least, it is through fantasy play that youngsters develop their sense of humor, practice empathy, and celebrate compassion.

Everyone senses on some level that the ability to be spontaneous and to play is a basic need and an important characteristic of healthy human beings. However, not everyone can channel this force for ultimate health and happiness. Unfortunately, learning to play is something we must do as children; if we do not learn how to play as youngsters, often it is a skill that cannot be learned as an adult. As parents and caregivers of young children, I urge you to teach your baby how to use her brain, body, ego, emotions, and imagination as vehicles for celebrating her higher self. When you teach your baby to play, you are showing her the path of intellectual, social, and emotional transformation—a path which ultimately leads to self-actualization!

© Instructional Fair • TS Denison

PLAYING

With Your

Newborn to Twelve-Month-Old

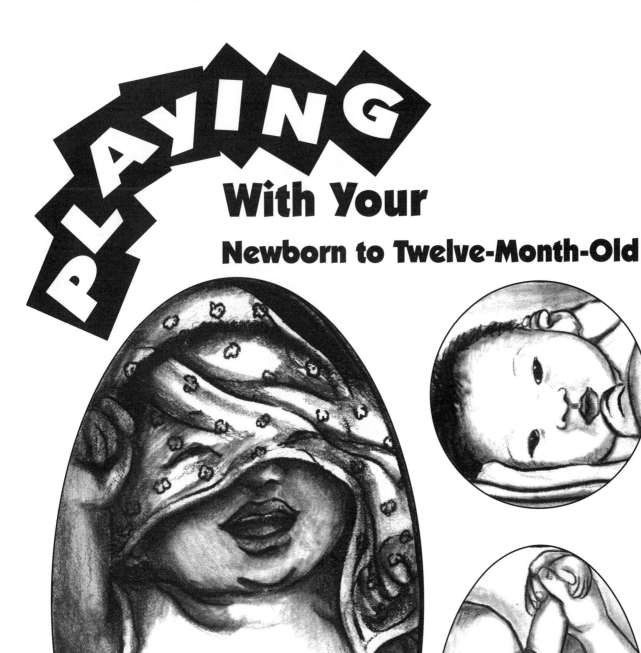

The Beginning

Playing with Your Newborn

 ### Contemplate

The brain of a fetus grows rapidly. In the first two months it grows from just a few cells into one of the most complex structures in nature. By the sixth month of pregnancy, a fetus can recognize its mother's voice and respond to movements. At birth, your baby's brain is still only partially formed. It is about one-third of its eventual size. Although the brain of a baby grows rapidly in the first few month, the child has no muscle control. Everything your baby does will be due to reflexes.

Reflexes are your baby's automatic response to a particular form of stimuli. Most reflexes have survival value, including breathing, swallowing, rooting, and sucking. Other reflexes may have had more survival qualities in the past. As the brain matures and there is a gradual increase in voluntary control, most newborn reflexes disappear within the first six months of life. There is a debate over whether reflexes for survival simply go away or if they become an integral and essential part of voluntary skills. Some newborn reflexes such as breathing and swallowing do not go away. Some reflexes only appear to go away. For example, the stepping reflex disappears due to lack of muscle strength. Although the stepping reflex stops, the mechanism responsible for it is used by the brain at a later age.

All babies are born grasping, reaching for something to hold onto—and that something is someone who loves them. For your baby, that someone is you!

Reflexes: Birth to Four Weeks

- Crying
- Breathing
- Sucking
- Swallowing
- Rooting
- Moro reflex
- Tonic neck reflex
- Grasping
- Walking/stepping
- Shutting out stimuli
- Protective reflexes
- Sleeping
- Smiling

© Instructional Fair • TS Denison

General Tips

In *The Common Sense Book of Baby and Child Care* (1946) Dr. Benjamin Spock wrote, "The more people have studied different methods of bringing up children, the more they have come to the conclusion that what good mothers and fathers instinctively feel like doing for their babies is the best after all." Because all babies are different, *you, the parent, will know what is best for your own baby.* The games in this book are activities designed to stimulate your baby. Although step-by-step directions are given, following them to the letter or understanding how they are developmentally sound is not nearly as important as being present and bonding with your baby. The more you play and talk to her, the quicker she will learn and the more secure she will feel.

We measure our ages from the moment we are born. However, your baby was already about 40 weeks old when she was born. Newborns have already undergone a great deal of physical development in the uterus. Socially and psychologically your baby began long before her birth. The age guidelines in this book are just that—guidelines. Each baby matures and reaches developmental stages in her own perfect timing. Trust that your baby is developing at exactly the right pace for her.

When your baby was born, the delivery nurse probably used a scoring system called "Apgar" to estimate your baby's general condition. The test is to measure heartbeat rate, breathing, muscle tone, reflex response, and color. The test is not an indicator of how intelligent your baby is or how healthy she is, but rather it is used to alert the hospital staff if an infant's responses are not normal—if she needs assistance adapting to her new environment. At birth, babies are immediately tested for newborn reflexes:

- ◆ Sucking
- ◆ Standing
- ◆ "Walking"
- ◆ Gripping

In the first month, the only way your newborn can relate to the world is through her reflexes. The only way she can communicate is through her crying. Although it may seem like she is not learning much, within the first few months of life, your baby will form a basic philosophy of life. Depending on how you treat her, she will decide if she should trust or distrust the world and if she is worthy of love.

Stimulating your newborn is important for her emotional development. You can stimulate her with contact and also by providing appropriate toys including:

- ◆ Musical mobile hung over the crib
- ◆ Crib that rocks from side to side
- ◆ Pacifier (if she wants one)
- ◆ Soft cuddly toy to be placed in the crib while she sleeps
- ◆ Plastic mirror attached to the side of the crib

*Playing with Your* **Newborn**

Cry Language

An infant crying in the night;
An infant crying for the light;
And with no language but a cry.
　　　　　　—Alfred Lord Tennyson

Overture

Infancy is a word that comes from a Latin term "infantia" which means an inability to speak. Most often the first sound a parent hears her baby make is when he cries at birth. Crying is the only way your baby has to tell you when he needs or wants something. Listen carefully, and you will hear that your baby has a variety of crying techniques.

Performance

Play: To help you learn your baby's cry language, pay close attention to each different cry. Soon you will be able to distinguish between his different cries and learn how to meet the needs indicated by each one.

What you will need: Notebook, pencil

How to play: For a day or two, note the different kinds of cries your baby has including any of the following:

- A piercing, painful-sounding cry
- A bored, hollow cry
- Short and low-pitched cry
- Beginning suddenly and getting louder and louder cry
- High-pitched shriek followed by long pauses
- A demanding, urgent cry
- A rhythmic but not urgent cry
- Rising and falling cry
- A flat wailing
- Silent sobbing

Note what it is that you do that makes your baby stop crying. Do you see a pattern? Does a short and low-pitched cry mean he is hungry? Does a flat wail mean he is sleepy and wants to sleep? Learn your baby's crying language.

Finale

Always respond quickly to your baby's crying. Your attentiveness to his needs will send a clear message that he is your priority. To find out which method your baby enjoys—which one quiets his crying, experiment with a variety of ways of calming your baby when he cries:

- Rock him and stroke his head or pat his back.
- Wrap him snugly in a blanket so he feels secure.
- Sing a lullaby.
- Walk around with him in your arms or take a ride in the car.
- Play soft music to soothe him.

Encore

If, sometimes, your baby is warm, dry, and not hungry but still cries, remember: crying meets several useful purposes. Crying helps your baby shut out the sensations that may be too intense for him and helps him release tension.

© Instructional Fair • TS Denison

Relaxed Breathing

A simple child, that lightly draws its breath,
And feels its life in every limb . . .
—William Wordsworth

Overture

At birth, your baby underwent a sudden change in environment. She had to take her first breath. It was at that moment that air first passed in and out of her lungs. It is probably the first time you heard her cry. For some infants, adjusting to the world outside the womb can be stressful.

Performance

Play: To give your baby an opportunity to relax and adjust to her new environment, model relaxation techniques.

What you will need: No special equipment is needed for this activity.

How to play: When you are nursing or feeding your newborn, take deep breathes. Relax and let go. Use the feeding times each day to stop and be still. If you are anxious and in a hurry to finish feeding your newborn, she will sense your anxiety. On the other hand, if you treasure the quiet moments that you spend nourishing her, she will feel loved and cherished. Remember, when you are feeding your baby, you have her undivided attention. She will most likely spend the time gazing into your face. If she reads love and acceptance in your smile, she will know she is cherished.

Finale

To reinforce your own relaxation during feeding, use that time to practice deep breathing techniques. As you inhale say to yourself, "Relax." As you exhale, repeat "Relax." Do that ten times. Then make a special effort to slow down your breathing while you are feeding your baby. Soon she will sense your relaxed state, and it will have a calming affect on her.

Encore

Practice various relaxation techniques on the baby to see which ones soothe her and help her fall asleep.

- With thumb and index finger, gently massage her tiny shoulders and neck.
- Use two fingers to gently rub lotion on her back.
- With one finger, gently stroke her forehead as you rock her.
- Use lotion to gently massage her feet and legs.
- Model slow, deep breathing for her.
- Rub her tummy gently.
- Place one finger on her chest over her heart and message gently.
- When you burp her, gently rub her whole back with the palm of your hand.

Language of Love

Dost thou not see my baby at my breast,
That sucks the nurse asleep?
—Shakespeare

Overture

Watch, and you will see that when your newborn's lips, mucous membranes of his mouth, or soft palate are stimulated he will begin to suck. Most babies want to suckle as soon as they are born. The sucking reflex is strong, but at the same time, it involves a complicated set of movements and needs to be coordinated with both swallowing and breathing.

Performance

Play: When suckling or feeding your baby, it is the perfect time to make pleasant cooing sounds to him. Play "Language of Love."
What you will need: No special equipment is needed for this activity.
How to play: While you are nursing or feeding your baby a bottle, you have a clear view of his face. At the same time, he can see your face. Use the language of love, communicated through pleasant sounds, to tell your baby he is cherished. Since he does not understand words anyway, you do not always have to communicate with words. He is more tuned into the pitch and tone of your voice. Try sounds of a bird cooing or make the sounds of a babbling brook, whistle, or hum. Choose a sound that you like to make and one that will be soothing to your baby. When you hear your baby making pleasant sounds, echo the sound back to him. Communicating your love on this level will be emotionally satisfying for your newborn. When you goo-goo-gaga back to him, he will have a powerful sense of communicating and connecting with you.

Finale

There is nothing quite like a baby to turn grown-ups into ahhhs and sighs. The awesomeness of your newborn will make most of those who see him want to respond in a positive, verbal way. Remember what people say about your newborn. Keep a notebook of compliments given your baby by family and friends. Then read your newborn the nice things that are being said about him. He will not understand the words, but he may internalize the messages of acceptance and love. Examples:
- ◆ Uncle Andy says you have gorgeous red hair.
- ◆ Your daddy thinks your skin is like pink silk.
- ◆ Sister says your beautiful brown eyes are as big as donuts.

Encore

Babies are born with a need to suck. This reflex is a very important response because not only does it keep the baby eating, the baby enjoys it immensely. When not sucking a bottle or breast, infants will suck on a pacifier, thumb, or fist. Make sure your baby has his sucking needs met. If he needs a pacifier, make sure he has one. Do not be alarmed at thumb sucking. Babies who suck their thumbs grow up to be children who can meet their own needs.

 © Instructional Fair • TS Denison

Time to Eat

Nimble and sweetly recommends itself
Unto our gentle senses.
                    —Shakespeare

Overture

Watch your newborn when she is hungry. She will turn her head toward stimuli and "root" in search of something to eat. If nothing is there, she may raise her hand to her mouth to suck on her fist or fingers. Hand-to-mouth reflex is called the "Babkin reflex." If you stroke your newborn's cheek or put a finger in the palm of her hand, she will bring her fist to mouth and suck on it.

Performance

Play: To help encourage your baby to search out and find the source of her food supply, play "Time to Eat."

What you will need: Warm milk

How to play: Before beginning to nurse or giving her a bottle, stroke a finger against her cheek near her mouth. She will turn toward the object, and if she makes contact with her lips, she will open her mouth and begin to suck. Rooting should always be followed with food. If you stimulate her rooting reflex and food does not follow, she may become very frustrated. When she turns her head rooting for food say, "Time to eat" (or any other verbal cue you choose). If the verbal cue "time to eat" is always followed by food, she will have learned another way of knowing when it is time to eat.

Finale

Your newborn will turn her head in response to stimuli besides touch. If you stand beside your baby's crib, out of sight, and speak softly she will probably turn her head toward the sound of your voice. This is good practice for your newborn. Speak softly. Watch how she turns her head toward the sound of your voice. Although generally speaking, newborns respond best to the sound of human voices, stimulate your baby's head turning with other sounds besides your voice including:

◆ Ring a little bell.
◆ Clap lightly.
◆ Play a music box.
◆ Whistle a little tune, sing a lullaby, or click your tongue.

Encore

On other occasions, get her to move her head in different directions as a stimuli response to visual cues. Six to ten inches (15–25 cm) away from your newborn, move a flashlight to slowly project a light through the field of view. Watch her try to follow the light by moving her head from side to side and letting her eyes wander. Find out what kinds of things get and hold your newborn's attention. Six to ten inches (15–25 cm) away from your baby's eyes:

◆ Try moving something black or dark colored.
◆ Try moving something that flutters like shiny streamers.
◆ Have different members of the family make gestures to see which ones she responds to by following their movements.

Flash the Light

All psychical acts without exception, if they are not complicated
by elements of emotion . . . develop by way of reflex.
—Ivan Mikhailovich Sechenov

Overture

Watch when your baby's head shifts positions abruptly or falls backward or if he is startled by something loud or abrupt. He will most likely throw out his arms and legs and extend his neck, then rapidly bring his limbs back together and begin to cry. This reflex is called the "Moro reflex." A baby who can habituate—decrease his level of responsiveness when stimuli are presented repeatedly—will have a built-in safeguard against over stimulation.

Performance

Exercise: To give your newborn an opportunity to learn how to habituate stimuli, play "Flash the Light."

What you will need: Flashlight

How to play: While your newborn is asleep, for a brief second, shine a flashlight through his closed eyelids. After the initial startle, he will settle down. Then flash the light again. After the initial response and he quiets down, flash the light again. Repeat about a dozen times. The first few times your baby may be startled and move his whole body. His arms and legs may jump. But each time you flash the light, the response should lessen until at the end there should be no response at all. Your newborn can habituate stimuli when:

◆ He no longer responds to the light on closed eyelids.
◆ There is little or no body movement.
◆ His breathing is deep and regular.
◆ His face is softened and whole body is relaxed.
◆ Further flashes of light gets no response at all.

Finale

To help your newborn learn how to shut out auditory stimuli, try these sleep tests to teach habituation to negative/disturbing stimuli:

◆ Shake a rattle 10 inches (25 cm) away from his ear. He should start to habituate by the fourth or fifth rattle and may be completely habituated by the tenth rattle.
◆ Ring a small bell for a one second burst. Your baby should habituate well between the fourth to tenth trial.

Encore

Failure to shut out external stimuli while sleeping may indicate a hypersensitive baby. A hypersensitive baby may require protected environments including:

◆ Quiet room with subdued light
◆ Low pitched, soft voices
◆ Gentle, easy visual or tactile stimuli
◆ Stimuli limited to one at a time

 © Instructional Fair • TS Denison

Peekaboo

*Beware lest you lose the substance
by grasping at the shadow.*
—Aesop

Overture

Watch your newborn when she is resting on her back. If she is startled, you may observe the "tonic neck reflex" (fencing reflex). If your baby's head is rotated to the left, the left arm will stretch into extension, and the right arm will flex up above head. The opposite reaction occurs when the head is rotated to the right side.

Performance

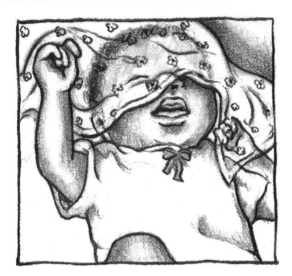

Play: To help your newborn practice protective reflexes, play "Peekaboo."

What you will need: Lightweight, transparent scarf

How to play: Place your newborn on her back. Place the scarf over her eyes and nose. Initially she will thrash about. Even though her airway is not obstructed, she will arch her head, turn from side to side, and try to throw off the cloth. She may use her hands to push or pull off the scarf. The head arching and the hands coming up to push off the scarf are examples of protective reflexes. After a couple seconds, pull off the scarf and say "Peekaboo." Repeat several times.

Finale

You can play games to strengthen your baby's response to pleasant sounds. Lie your baby on her back. Hold a musical toy to one side of her within her reach. Watch her arm stretch out as she turns her head to see what is making the melody. Look at the arm on the opposite side of her body. Is it curled up? Move the toy to the other side of her body. Watch as she turns her head and moves her arms. To be able to move one arm to reach while the other arm is suppressed is important as your baby develops a dominant side for coordinated activity.

Encore

Besides stimulating your newborn with a sound on one or the other side of her body, try other sensory stimuli such as:

- ◆ Something that has a pleasant aroma (flower or mother's perfume)
- ◆ Something shining (flashlight or nightlight)
- ◆ Something moving (rolling ball)
- ◆ Something that softly touches her (scarf or breeze)

Squeeze Me

This living hand, now warm and capable
Of earnest grasping . . .
—John Keats

Overture

Watch as you stroke the palm of your baby's hand; he will immediately grip your finger. Watch as you stroke the sole of his foot; he will flex as the toes curl tightly. From the moment of birth, babies have strong hand and toe grasps.

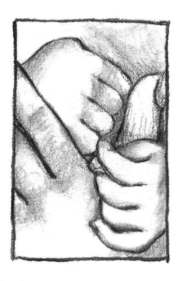

Performance

Exercise: To reinforce your infant's grasp, try grasping his fingers the same way he grasps yours. Play "Squeeze Me."

What you will need: No special equipment is needed for this activity.

How to play: Place your index finger in your baby's hand, and he will grasp onto it tightly. Remove your finger from his grasp, and then gently grasp his tiny index finger. One at a time, grasp each of his fingers gently. Look at his tiny fingernails. Tell him how beautiful his hands are. Try other grasping techniques:

◆ Grasp his whole hand in your hand.
◆ Put his two hands together and grasp them gently.
◆ Grasp his tiny thumbs one at a time.
◆ Grasp his wrist.

Finale

Physical contact with your baby will make him feel safe and loved. Use the grasp hold to stimulate his legs, feet, and toes. Gently squeeze his tiny legs. Squeeze his little feet. Gently press an index finger on the bottom of each tiny toe. Touching your baby will ground him and outline his body for him. Being held helps him feel like he belongs, and he will experience good feelings from kisses and hugs.

Encore

If contact is denied or reduced in the early weeks of a baby's life, it will negatively affect the baby's emotional well being. There is a critical, sensitive period immediately after birth when a parent is particularly able to form a close relationship with the baby. In the first few weeks of your baby's life, pay special attention to making touching contact. Stroke, pat, rub, hug, kiss, and hold your baby as much as possible.

 © Instructional Fair • TS Denison

Bicycle Pedaling

Light of step and heart was she.
—Walter de la Mare

Overture

Hold your baby upright, carefully supporting her head, place her feet on a firm surface. Supporting reflexes will cause her to extend her legs and try to bear her own weight. Hold her in an upright position with the upper part of her feet touching the edge of a table, and she will lift her feet almost as if trying to step over the table. This is the stepping reflex.

Performance

Exercise: To help your newborn strengthen her legs, use the bicycle pedaling exercise.

What you will need: No special equipment is needed for this exercise.

How to play: Place your baby on the floor on her back. Hold each of her feet in one of your hands. Very slowly and gently pedal her legs as if she is riding a bike. Then move the legs in a movement of straightening and bending together. Exercise legs in these two ways about a dozen times each. Don't over exercise your newborn. Her muscles are not used to any kind of activity yet. Do this gentle exercising each day the first few months.

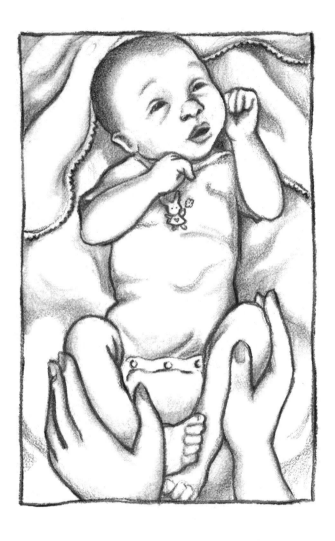

Finale

To exercise the upper half of her body, exercise her arms as you did her legs. Place your baby on her back. Hold each hand in one of your hands. Bring her hands apart and place them out straight out on the floor. Next, bring her hands together in the air as if she is clapping. Repeat about a dozen times. Also stretch baby's arms up over her head so that her hands touch. Then bring each arm down to make a wide circle, ending with her hands resting at her sides. Also exercise her arms in both of these ways a few times each day for the first few months.

Encore

Another way of exercising baby is to place objects in her grasp that will stimulate her to reach and stretch. She will bring up her own arms to reach for an object. A musical mobile that hangs over her crib might stimulate her to reach for the circling objects. Babies also exercise themselves when they thrash around or wail.

Crawl and Swim

A pretty Babe all burning bright did in the air appear.
—Robert Southwell

Overture

Watch your newborn's movements the first few days—they will be very jerky. His chin may quiver and tremble. He may startle easily when he hears a loud sound or is moved suddenly. By the end of the first month his nervous system will mature, his muscle control will improve, and his movements will become smoother.

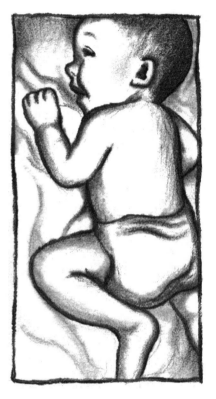

Performance

Exercise: To help your newborn move in smooth ways, play "Crawl and Swim."

What you will need: No special equipment is needed for this exercise.

How to play: Two newborn reflexes that you can use to exercise your baby are the crawling and swimming reflexes. The crawling reflex can be seen if you place your newborn on his abdomen. He will flex his legs under him and try to crawl. If you stroke along the side of his spine while he is held (place your hand under his belly to hold him), he will flex his whole body to the side that is stroked. This is known as the "Gallant response" (or swimming reflex). Try these two activities with your baby.

Finale

Additional ways to exercise his body while he is resting on his stomach include:

- ◆ Using your hands to guide his feet in a crawling movement.
- ◆ Moving his arms as if in a butterfly swimming stroke.
- ◆ Lifting him slightly so he will pull his knees and arms in as if to help support his own weight; then place him back flat on his stomach.
- ◆ Using your hands gently to turn his head from side to side.
- ◆ Gently and slowly straighten out each leg; then let him curl it back up where he is comfortable again.

Encore

After the first month, your baby's neck muscles will develop rapidly and give him much more control over his head movement. Use a rattle to stimulate his curiosity on either side of his body so he will turn his head. The lifting and turning of his head will strengthen his neck muscles. If he cannot lift his head to turn it, wait a few weeks to introduce this exercise.

 © Instructional Fair • TS Denison

Sleeping

Rock-a-bye Baby in a treetop.
—Traditional Rhyme

Overture

There are two states of sleep for newborns: One state is deep sleep; one state is light sleep. Watch your newborn in deep sleep, and you will see her lying quietly without moving. If she is sleeping but moving around, she is in light sleep.

Performance

Play: To help your baby begin sleeping longer at night, avoid long late-in-the-day naps by keeping her awake with games.

What you will need: Rattles, stuffed toys, musical toys, etc.

How to play: These quick games to stimulate your newborn and keep her awake should be played for just a few minutes at a time. Infants quickly lose interest in a game and need new stimuli to hold interest. Here are some games to play while she is resting on her back:

♦ Shake a rattle above her and within her grasp so she will reach for it.
♦ Hang a beach ball from the ceiling close enough for her to reach.
♦ Put a pinwheel on the side of her crib so it will spin in a breeze.
♦ Show her black and white pictures with high contrast patterns like a dart board target.
♦ Show her large black and white photographs of family members.

Finale

Use games to stimulate her while she is resting in your lap including:

♦ Make silly faces.
♦ Bring your hand from a distance of 10 inches (25 cm) down to her chin and touch it; repeat moving back and forth.
♦ Make eye contact and then make silly sounds.
♦ Make a sound as you gently tweak her nose.
♦ Hold a soft toy in front of her, bring it into her tummy, and rub her with it.

Encore

In the beginning, your infant will not know the difference between night and day, and her stomach will only hold enough food for three or four hours. At least in the first few weeks, around-the-clock feeding will interrupt her sleep. The less you stimulate her during her feedings, the more quickly she will fall back to sleep. Consider these:

♦ Do not let her cry very long when she calls to you; crying for a long time will waken her completely.
♦ Do not turn on a light; just use a night-light.
♦ Do not move her from room to room; nurse or feed her in her bedroom next to her crib where you can gently place her when she falls asleep.
♦ Do not talk to her; instead, hum or sing very softly while rocking, but do not carry on a loud conversation.

Being Awake

Was it a vision, or a waking dream?
. . . Do I wake or sleep?
—John Keats

Overture

Watch your baby, and you will see six states of consciousness: deep sleep, light sleep, and four stages of being awake:

- **Semi-Alert**—Drowsiness, eyes start to close and he may doze; this short-lived state is one that occurs frequently as the infant rouses or returns to sleep.
- **Wide-Awake and Alert**—His eyes are open wide, face bright, and body quiet.
- **Fussy, Active Alertness**—May thrash around with jerky movements; he may go into an uncontrolled crying state.
- **Crying**—Many different kinds of crying can be demonstrated; he may move his whole body in a very disorganized way.

Performance

Play: To stimulate your infant's alertness, play games that will interest his visual and hearing senses.
What you will need: Paper plate puppet made from a white plate with simple, black line facial features: eyes, nose, mouth. Draw spots for the eyes and nose and a curved line for the mouth.
How to play: Place your baby in your lap. Hold up the paper plate puppet about 10 inches (25 cm) from his eyes. Make a silly sound. Then take the puppet away. Smile at your baby. Then make the same silly sound. Does the sound trigger his curiosity to see the face again? Show him the paper plate puppet each time you make the sound. Then show him the puppet without making a sound. Does he try to make a sound when he sees the puppet face?

Finale

Play games that will stimulate his sense of smell. Put pleasant smelling foods on a table. Sit down next to the table holding the baby in your lap. One at a time, sniff a food, and then put it near the baby's nose so he can smell it, too. Say something like this: "Doesn't that smell good? Chocolate cookie."
Examples of foods infants usually enjoy sniffing:

- Banana
- Orange
- Gingersnap cookie
- Apple slice

Encore

An infant is very sensitive to touch and the way he is handled. He will prefer soft flannel or satin clothing and blankets. Play games that will stimulate his sense of touch. Cut 6-inch (15-cm) squares of a variety of textured materials: velvet, fur, flannel, tweed, terry cloth, and silk. Place baby on his back on a blanket without socks. Touch the bottom of his feet with each texture. Let him use his fingers to explore the textures, too. On other occasions, use a warm wet sponge and a dry towel to stimulate the bottoms of his feet. Alternate the experiences.

© Instructional Fair • TS Denison

Smiling

I would see a little Torquatus,
stretching his baby hands from his mother's lap,
smile a sweet smile at his father with lips half parted.
—Gaius Valerius Catullus

Overture

Watch your baby, and you may be surprised to see her first smiles or even hear that very first giggle. Smiling and giggling often begin during sleep. Sometime between the first and third months, your baby may begin to grin back at you during her alert periods.

Performance

Play: To encourage your newborn to smile, smile at your baby often and soon she will be smiling back at you.
What you will need: Light, transparent scarf
How to play: Lay the baby in your lap facing up. Hold the scarf about 10 in. (25 cm) from her face. Slowly lower it onto her face, pull it off quickly, and say "Peekaboo!" Smile at your baby. If your baby enjoys the game, repeat several times.

Finale

Smiles are reassuring for babies. To reinforce smiling, smile at your baby often, including:
◆ First thing in the morning and when she wakes up from her nap, greet her with a smile.
◆ Smile and gaze into your baby's face when you are feeding her.
◆ While you are diapering her, smile at her to let her know you do not mind taking good care of her.
◆ When she stops crying, smile a big smile to let her know you are happy she has stopped crying.
◆ Return all of her smiles with a smile.

Encore

Whether you know it or not, your infant is looking to you to know if the world is a positive and good place, or a negative and bad place. If you are feeling anxious, your baby will feel the tension. Of course, you will need to have and express your negative feelings, but you can let your baby know it is not her fault that you are sad, angry, or tired by smiling at her and never directing your anger at her.

Teaching Trust

A little work, a little play,
To keep us going—and so, good day!
A little trust that when we die
We reap our sowing! and so—good-bye!
—George du Maurier

Overture

The developmental task for the early stage of infancy is that of forming a basic philosophy of life. In the first days of his life, your baby will decide if he can trust or distrust; because of the way he is treated now, some personal traits will be affected.

Performance

Activity: To teach your newborn to trust, there are four main factors: feeding, touching, bonding, and stimulating. Meeting all four of these needs will give your baby a secure feeling.

What you will need: No special equipment is needed for this activity.

How to play: Feeding is the perfect time to reinforce all four factors of trust. Here are some ways to do that:

◆ Answer your newborn's cry for food as soon as he lets you know he is hungry.
◆ As you are feeding your baby, touch his face gently with the tip of your index finger.
◆ Bond with him by making eye contact as you are feeding him.
◆ Stimulate him by speaking to him of your love and adoration for him.

Finale

Eye contact during feeding is an excellent way to bond. Do not look around the room and think about the dust on the furniture or the floor that needs to be vacuumed. The laundry that needs folding can wait. The precious time you have with your newborn will slip away too soon. Remember, your newborn will only be the age he is today for one day. Tomorrow he will be a day older, and with each new day he will grow and change. Enjoy this very moment. Be here and now with your baby.

Encore

It does not matter what you say or sing to your newborn. When you pay attention to your baby—cuddle, hug, and kiss him—you are saying, "I love you." And when you teach him that you love him, you are instilling trust in him.

© Instructional Fair • TS Denison

Keeping Track

Milestone	Date	Comments
Cries when hungry, in pain, or needs attention		
Takes first breath when born		
Demonstrates the sucking reflex		
Demonstrates the rooting reflex		
Responds to sound and visual stimuli		
Learns to shut out stimuli		
Demonstrates protective reflexes		
Demonstrates the grasping reflex		
Demonstrates the supporting reflexes		
Muscle control becomes more smooth		
Exhibits the two stages of sleep		
Exhibits the four stages of alertness		
May begin to smile		

Little Changes

Playing with Your One-Month-Old

Contemplate

Your baby will give you many wonderful gifts that no one else can ever give you, and you, in turn, will give your baby what he needs to survive, grow, and someday become an independent human being. Among the gifts your baby will give you are:

◆ **Unconditional love**—From the moment your baby is born, he will believe you are the center of the universe.

◆ **Trust**—Your baby believes that everything you do and say is truth. The way you treat your baby is the way he believes he deserves to be treated.

◆ **Excitement**—By watching your baby discover the world, you will begin to see things in a new, fresh light. Everything will seem more awesome as you explore the world together.

◆ **Purpose**—Your baby will need you as no one else has ever needed you before now. His life and happiness rests in your hands.

The gifts you will give your baby include:

◆ **Unconditional love**—Acceptance of your baby as a unique individual with a right to his basic nature, will send him a clear message of your unconditional love.

◆ **A sense of belonging**—By playing with your baby, adhering to family rituals, and celebrating life you will give your baby the feeling of belonging. He will gain the pride that comes from being an intrinsic part of a family.

◆ **Positive self-esteem**—As you praise your baby, hug and kiss him, and treasure his accomplishments, you child will know by your gentle touches and careful listening that you believe that he is worthwhile.

◆ **Values**—By modeling integrity and principles that are important to you as an individual, you are teaching your child the belief system he will need to be a good citizen and someday a good partner and parent.

Milestones: Four to Eight Weeks

◆ Will be comforted by rocking, singing, and other vibrations
◆ Will be comforted by sucking
◆ May have a fussy period toward the end of each day
◆ Will gain comfort from cuddling and swaddling
◆ Will begin to smile
◆ Will recognize mother's voice and may recognize other familiar voices
◆ Will begin to make sounds
◆ Will move his eyes around in all directions
◆ Will follow an object held within range of his vision with his eyes
◆ Will notice and watch his own feet and hands
◆ Will respond to a rattle when shaken within range of his hearing
◆ Will begin to be able to control his own head
◆ Will begin to kick purposefully

 ## General Tips

It is especially important for your baby's later development that she have a stimulating environment today. Every day take a few minutes to play games that will stimulate all of her senses.

To **stimulate her auditory environment**, talk to her, play music for her, and provide musical instruments like bells and mobiles for her to see and touch and hear.

To **stimulate her visually**, enter her range of vision which in the early months is only 10–18 inches (25–46 cm). When you talk to her, put your face near hers. When you show her toys, place them where she can see them.

Stimulate her by touches. Hugs, pats, kisses, and rocking will ground her and make her feel loved. Moving about while she is in your arms will stimulate her, too. Dance with her, take her for walks, and push her in a carriage or stroller.

Infants **prefer sweet aromas** to any others. At birth, a baby can identify the smell of her own mother's milk. A mother's perfume holds significance for babies and sometimes a drop of perfume (if family members do not have allergies) on your baby's pillow will make her feel close to you while she sleeps.

Since infants only drink milk, stimulating her **sense of taste** is not something you can do much about this first month. But she can be satisfied orally by having a pacifier or being allowed to suck her thumb for comfort. Her need to eat will seem urgent to her, so feed your baby as soon as she cries for food.

Appropriate toys for stimulating a one-month-old:
- ◆ Musical mobile hung over her crib
- ◆ Soft, cuddly toys
- ◆ Rattles that she can watch you shake
- ◆ Jingle bells sewed securely to her socks
- ◆ Black and white photographs of people, designs, and objects
- ◆ Basic musical instruments to hear and touch

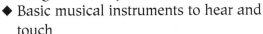

Rock-a-Bye, Baby

Rock-a-by, baby, thy cradle is green.
Father's a nobleman, mother's a queen.
—Traditional Rhyme

Overture

Most tiny babies enjoy the feeling of being secure and bundled up while rocked back and forth. Holding and rocking your baby will bring him much comfort. It has been said that touch is "the language of love." Babies are born helpless. Through your loving kindness you are giving him exactly what he needs most—gentle touches. Through your touches you communicate the caring and love he needs for emotional growth.

Performance

Play: To help your baby fall asleep and feel secure, spend time rocking him.
What you will need: Rocking chair or you may stand while holding your baby
How to play: Perhaps the most widely used means of calming a baby in our culture (beyond feeding) is through movement. Hold your baby so his chest rests on yours. Rock your baby to the beat of your heart. Listen for the beat of his heartbeat. Rock to the rhythm of two beating hearts.

Finale

Rhythmical sounds, as well as movements, are soothing for infants. The lullaby is probably as old as human infancy. Most have a slow rhythm which is similar to the frequency with which cradles are rocked. Singing to babies while they are being rocked is soothing. Use a familiar tune like "Twinkle, Twinkle, Little Star" to help your baby relax.

Twinkle, twinkle, little star.
How I wonder what you are.
Up above the world so high,
Like a diamond in the sky.
Twinkle, twinkle, little star,
How I wonder what you are.

Or make up an original personalized verse for the same tune.

Twinkle, twinkle, little boy (girl).
How I love who you are.
Curled up in my arms so still,
Like a purring kitten will.
Twinkle, twinkle, little boy (girl).
You bring your mama much joy!

Encore

The rhythmic motion of an automatic swing, a buggy ride, or sitting on top of a washer or dryer in an infant seat may be comforting for your baby. Some babies respond in a relaxed way to low-pitched steady noises such as vaporizers, fans, or recordings of winds or oceans. Some babies will fall asleep instantly when strapped in a car seat and taken for a ride. Experiment with different rhythmic sounds and movements to see which ones your baby prefers.

 © Instructional Fair • TS Denison

It's a Comfort

Sucking is a healthy self-comforting pattern.
—T. Berry Brazelton, M.D.

Overture ....

Watch, and you will see that your baby has learned how to get her thumb or fist to her mouth. It is a stressful world for an infant. Even at the early age of four to eight weeks, your baby will begin meeting her own needs.

Performance ....

Activity: To give your baby an opportunity to meet her own sucking needs, encourage her to use a pacifier, or allow her the freedom to suck her thumb or fist.
What you will need: Pacifier, thumb, fist, or nipple of an empty bottle
How to play: When your baby needs soothing, give her something to suck.

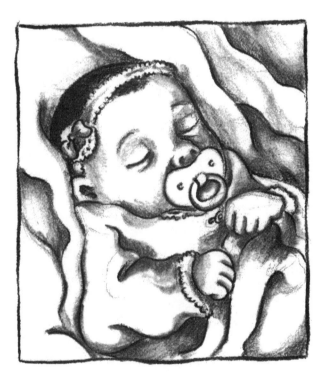

Finale ....

Sucking has a quieting effect. Often, babies will choose particular blankets or toys which they like to hold or stroke while they are sucking. Make sure your baby has a "lovie" that she naps and sleeps with. By the age of three or four the lovie toy may be disintegrating and the stuffing may be falling out, but your child may still prefer that particular "lovie" to use while she sucks. Objects that bring comfort to many babies include:

- ◆ Small blanket with a satin trim around the edge
- ◆ Rag doll with simple, smiling face
- ◆ Small, soft teddy bear
- ◆ Windup musical toy

Encore ....

Some parents feel that if their baby needs a comforter, it is a failure on their part to keep the baby happy. Using a comfort toy as a transitional object between the physical presence of the mother and the mental image of her that the baby will need during her absences is a good thing. Helping your baby find ways of meeting her own needs is a positive step toward her eventual independence. Having a lovie object that the baby knows is hers and under her control will empower her. You can help your baby select her lovie. Place several possibilities in the crib near your baby. Watch to see which one she reaches for and grabs onto. It may take her awhile to make a choice, but once she does, it will bring her comfort for many days to come.

What's All the Fuss?

Lulla, lulla, lullaby,
Softly sleep, my baby;
Lulla, lulla, lullaby,
Soft, soft, my baby.
—Traditional Rhyme

Overture

Watch your month-old baby in the late afternoons. You may notice that he has a fussy period. Expecting this behavior and understanding its value for your infant will spare you unnecessary panic and anxiety. Allowing your baby to fuss at the end of each day is important to his emotional well-being.

Performance

Activity: When your baby gets fussy at the end of the day, try some maneuvers to calm him, but do not do too much or you may just stimulate him more.

What you will need: No special equipment is needed for this activity.

How to play: Vary your handling and try out a variety of things to make sure your baby does not really need you to meet a need. Then if several of the following do not soothe him, let him fuss for awhile.
- Pick him up.
- Walk around with him in your arms.
- Cuddle and rock him.
- Feed him or give him warm water to drink.
- Change his diaper.

Finale

How long should you let a baby fuss? Ten or fifteen minutes is enough. Then give him some warm water to drink because he will have swallowed some air while he was crying. Burp him. If he still fusses, put him down again for another ten or fifteen minutes followed by warm water and burping again. Repeat several more times if needed. Most babies do not fuss more than an hour or two.

Encore

An immature nervous system can take in and utilize only so much stimuli in one day. As the day progresses, an overload of the nervous system causes babies to sleep shorter lengths of time and become less able to shut out stimuli. As if to blow off steam, a fussy period allows the baby's nervous system to release and reorganize. After your baby has a fussy time, he will be able to sleep in a relaxed state for a longer time.

 © Instructional Fair • TS Denison

Let's Dance

Dance with your daddy, my little baby.
Dance with your mommy, my little lamb.
—Traditional Rhyme

Overture

Swaddling (wrapping baby snugly) and holding your baby close may soothe her. Infants need to be cuddled and loved as much as they need to be fed and changed. The more you hold your baby, the more quickly you will learn to interpret her feelings and needs. Watch, and you will see your baby begin to use body movements to communicate.

Performance

Play: To incorporate some music and snuggling into your day with your baby, play "Let's Dance."
What you will need: Slow, jazz music
How to play: Wrap the baby in a lightweight blanket (swaddle). Then hold her close to your chest. Besides slow dancing, move around to the rhythm of the music with a variety of dance steps including:

◆ Classical music
◆ Big band hits from the 1940s
◆ Music from Disney movies
◆ Lullabies created for sleepy babies

Finale

Besides cuddling your baby and dancing to music, cuddle her and try other movements to lull her into a relaxed state:

◆ Move as if drifting on a raft at sea.
◆ Move as if wearing ice skates.
◆ Move as if downhill skiing.
◆ Move as if floating in water.
◆ Move as if being blown by the wind.

Encore

Used with care, swaddling can be used to make your baby feel secure. By wrapping an infant in a sheet or blanket, a fretful child can be helped into a peaceful sleep. For this technique to be successful, it is important to begin using it during the first few weeks of life. If not begun until a child is several months old, a baby will often fight against any restriction she is not used to.

Smile, Baby, Smile!

Smile, Baby, smile,
Baby wants to smile awhile.

Overture..

Sometime during the first few months, you will witness your baby's first true smile. Watch your baby; soon you will see that he recognizes you and will give you a smile. Smiling will become his second way—crying will still be his first way—of communicating with you.

Performance ....

Play: To reinforce your baby's smiling, play "Smile, Baby, Smile."

What you will need: No special equipment is needed to play this game.

How to play: When you are rocking and feeding your baby, say, "Smile, Baby, smile." Then give your baby a big smile. Touch his chin or playfully rub his tummy. When you say good night, give your baby a big smile. When your baby smiles at you first say, "Smile, Baby, smile" and smile back. When he gets used to associating the verbal request to "smile" and the act of smiling, you may be able to use it when he is crying or needs to be distracted in some way.

Finale ....

Use a smile to give your baby encouragement today, and it will last a lifetime. When you want to calm your baby, tell him how beautiful he is or express how much you love him and accompany the positive words with a smile. Smiling can become your nonverbal way of encouraging your baby. Teach him as an infant that a smile means positive things about how terrific he is; then as he grows up, when others smile at him, it will trigger a good message.

Encore ....

When your baby smiles at you, always smile back. This unspoken language of love will become an important part of his social and emotional development. Responding quickly and enthusiastically to his smiles will give him an opportunity to "speak" to you before he has acquired language.

 © Instructional Fair • TS Denison

Hello, Baby

Hello baby, my sweet friend
I've come to talk with you again.

Overture

By the end of the second month, your baby will spend a great deal of her waking hours watching and listening to those around her. Watch and you may notice your infant gazing at your face and smiling slightly at the sound of your voice. For infants, the human voice is the most interesting of all sounds.

Performance

Play: To help your baby learn to recognize familiar voices, play "Hello, Baby."

What you will need: No special equipment is needed for this activity.

How to play: When you enter the room where your baby is, greet her with "Hello, (baby's name)." When you are working in the room and your baby is in a crib or carrier, talk to her. Saying "Hello, (baby's name)" lets her know that you are aware of her presence and you want to communicate. It is said that to human beings, the sound of one's own name is among one's favorite sounds. Use your baby's name often every day. Other times to use her name include:

◆ After you have changed her—"(Baby's name) is dry and comfy again."
◆ When you are feeding her—"(Baby's name) is drinking her milk now."
◆ When siblings enter the room—"(Baby's name) sees (name of sibling)."
◆ When you are bathing her—"(Baby's name) is getting nice and clean."
◆ When you tell her good night—Good night, sweet (baby's name).

Finale

Play another listening game using your baby's name. Place your baby on her back. Walk around to one side of her and say "Hello (baby's name)." When she turns her head to look at you, say it again. Then walk around to the other side and repeat the exercise.

Encore

Pay attention to the way your baby responds to sounds. Loud sounds may still startle her. Watch to see if she becomes quiet and turns her head toward you when you talk to her. If she does not seem to respond to sounds around her, you may want to consider a hearing test. If your infant cannot hear well, it will interfere with her normal language development.

Goo, Goo, Gaga

Goo, goo, gaga,
Talkin' to my mama.

Overture

Listen to your baby and you will hear cooing and gurgling noises—he can now make some noises besides cries. Watch, and you will see how happy he is when sounds come from his mouth. He already knows that crying gets your attention. Soon he will learn that other sounds he makes can get your attention, too.

Performance

Play: To reinforce your baby's sounds, play "Goo, Goo, Gaga."
What you will need: No special equipment is needed to play this game.
How to play: Lay your baby in your lap. Make the "goo, goo, gaga" sound. Smile at your baby. Listen for him to make a sound. If he does, tell him how wonderful it is. Repeat the "goo, goo, gaga" sound. Pause to give him a chance to make a sound. Repeat this game on different days. Soon your baby will understand that you are having a conversation and try to make sounds back to you.

Finale

Familiar words, sounds, and voices will make your baby feel secure. You can use music to give security in many different ways including:

◆ A music box that you wind up for him to listen to while he is falling asleep will be reassuring.
◆ A musical mobile hung over his crib to watch and hear while he is falling asleep will be comforting.
◆ Classical CDs or audiotapes played during the day while he is awake will be soothing or stimulating depending upon the music.
◆ A special lullaby that you sing to him when he is fussy will be encouraging.

Encore

Show your baby interesting sounds you can make with your hands. Someday he will try to make the same sounds. Try some of these:

◆ Rubbing your hands together to make a quiet sound.
◆ Clapping softly with your hands, then holding his hands and clapping them together to make a sound.
◆ Drumming your hands on a table.
◆ Snap your fingers.
◆ With palms together, pressing the air out between your hands in a fast squeeze.
◆ Placing your hands near your baby's ears, and rubbing your fingers across your thumb repeatedly to make a quiet rubbing sound.

© Instructional Fair • TS Denison

Watch My Hands

Watch my hands,
Follow my fingers.

Overture

As your baby's eyesight is developing, she will enjoy watching interesting things. Around one month of age, her favorite patterns will be simple linear images such as stripes or a checkerboard. Your baby cannot distinguish colors yet, so black and white are the only colors she can see right now.

Performance

Play: To give your baby practice moving her eyes around in all directions, play "Watch My Hands."

What you will need: Black socks

How to play: Sit your baby in an infant seat. Put a black sock on each of your hands. Tuck your thumbs down so each sock makes a straight, thick dash. Place your hands about 18 in. (46 cm) from her face. Move your hands so the stripes are horizontal and then vertical. Rotate one hand so that one stripe is horizontal and the other is vertical. Then move both hands so the pattern is the reverse. Entertain your baby with the black socks until she gets bored with it.

Finale

Wearing the black socks on your hands, play other movement games including:

- ◆ Move your hands back about 18 in. (46 cm) to 1 yard (91 cm) from the baby. See if the baby can follow your hands.
- ◆ Try moving your hands in random patterns of up, down, and all around about 18 in. (46 cm) from her face to see if she follows with her eyes.
- ◆ Clap your hands together, apart, and together again.
- ◆ Move hands in circular patterns in the same direction. Then move them in a circular pattern in different directions.

Encore

Place tiny, black socks on your baby's hands, and see if she finds watching them interesting. If she does not like her hands in socks, try black mittens.

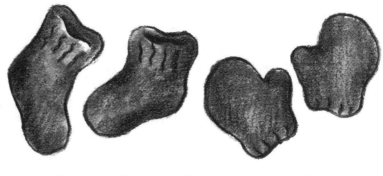

Follow the Ball

Currahoo, ccurr dhoo,
Love me, and I'll love you!
(Imitate a pigeon)
—Traditional Rhyme

Overture

Observe your baby while he is watching things, and you will see that his eyes can move around and follow objects better than he did a few weeks ago.

Performance

Play: To give your baby practice following an object with his eyes, play "Follow the Ball."

What you will need: A small, black rubber ball

How to play: Lay the baby in a carrier or infant seat. Hold the ball about 18 inches (46 cm) from his eyes. Move the ball in different patterns to see if he can follow it with his gaze including:

- ◆ Slowly move it in a pattern of small circular motions.
- ◆ Move it in the same small, circular pattern but increase the speed.
- ◆ Slowly move the ball back and forth in a horizontal line.
- ◆ Speed up the horizontal movement.
- ◆ Slowly move the ball up and down in a vertical line.
- ◆ Speed up the vertical movement.

Finale

Try slowly waving a black scarf in front of your baby's face. Wave it in circular patterns. Then slowly wave it in vertical and horizontal patterns. Play some music and wave the scarf to the music. After the game, tie the scarf near your baby where he can grab it with his hands or kick it with his feet.

Encore

As your baby gets better at holding his gaze, he will begin to stare at your eyes. At first he may look away when you gaze at him. Then after experiencing this game of staring, he will be able to extend the periods of direct eye contact. Each day look into his eyes and see if he can hold your gaze for longer periods of time. Talking to your baby while you hold his gaze will help him lengthen the time he stays focused.

© Instructional Fair • TS Denison

Tinker Bell Socks

Dance and caper, shake your legs.
Prance and skip, rattle your toes.
—Traditional Rhyme

Overture

Watch your baby, and you will see that she sometimes discovers that she can make things happen. Although she has a very short attention span and short-term memory, she will now begin to repeat behavior that causes certain things to happen.

Performance

Play: To enhance your baby's fun while watching her own feet, play "Tinker Bell Socks."

What you will need: Jingle bells, baby socks, thread and needle

How to play: Securely sew some jingle bells on the toes of your baby's socks. Put the socks on her. Sit her in a carrier or infant seat. Move her foot with your hand to ring the jingle bells. Repeat with the other foot. Play with the bells on her socks until she understands that kicking her feet will ring the bells.

Finale

Securely sew jingle bells to the fingers of mittens. Place the mittens on your baby. Let her discover that moving her hands will ring the jingle bells. With your hands, help her clap and wave. Move her hands in a variety of ways so she will see how movement causes the bells to ring. When finished with the activity, remove the mittens. Do not leave them on your baby's hands if you are not going to stay with your baby. On other occasions, sew jingle bells on clothes at knee and elbows so shaking her arms and legs will ring the bells.

Encore

You can stimulate your baby with a variety of household sounds. Some babies are afraid of the sound of vacuum sweepers and garbage disposals. Loud sounds may frighten her, while humming sounds such as a hair dryer may be soothing for her. Put your baby in a carrier or infant seat and take her around the house to different rooms. Demonstrate some of the sounds in the house. Talk about the sounds your baby is hearing and name each sound including:

- ◆ Doorbell
- ◆ Egg timer
- ◆ Clothes dryer
- ◆ CD player
- ◆ Computer printer

- ◆ Oven buzzer
- ◆ Hair dryer
- ◆ Ticking clock
- ◆ Blender set on low speed
- ◆ Telephone ringing

Shake and Rattle

I am glad, glad with all my heart.
No one can shake or rattle us apart.
—Traditional Rhyme

Overture

When only a few weeks old, a baby will begin to recognize familiar objects. Watch, and you will see your baby looking at new objects placed in his line of vision. He will probably prefer focusing his attention on the familiar things. Gazing at familiar objects may give your baby a feeling of security.

Performance

Play: To reinforce your baby's response to a rattle when it is shaken within his vision, play "Shake and Rattle."

What you will need: Baby rattle

How to play: Sit your baby in a carrier or infant seat. Hold a rattle about 18 inches (46 cm) from his face. Shake it three to seven times. Pause. Watch the baby's eyes to see if he is focused on the rattle. Shake it several times again. Each time you shake the rattle and pause, look to see if he is watching the rattle. Does the sound of the rattle get his attention? When you pause and stop the rattling sound, do his eyes immediately shift away? Use the rattle to stimulate his focus for a few minutes at a time.

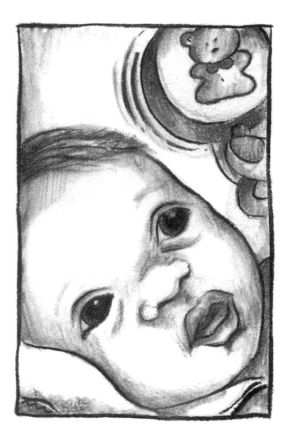

Finale

On other occasions, use rattles to reinforce your baby's focus. Shake the rattle to the left of his head. When he turns his head in the direction of the rattle, move it to the other side, and shake it again. Wait for him to find the rattle with his eyes. Then shake the rattle above his head. Watch to see if he can tell from where the sound is coming and if he can focus on it. Experiment to see from how far away he can focus on the rattle.

Encore

Your baby will not be able to grasp a rattle and shake it yet. Try pinning a rattle to the bottom of your baby's sock. Will he lift his leg and shake his foot? Does the rattle stimulate your baby to kick? Pin a rattle to his sleeve. Watch to see if he will move his arm to shake the rattle. If your baby finds this annoying and tries to get the rattle off his foot or sleeve, remove it and do not play this game.

© Instructional Fair • TS Denison

Look There!

Look ye there!
—Henry Fielding

Overture

Watch, and you will see that the more your baby sees and hears, the more she will want to see and hear. The stimulation your baby needs is not that of abstract mental information. She needs sensory stimulation and motor stimulation.

Performance

Play: To help your baby build muscles needed to control her own head, play "Look There!"

What you will need: Flashlight, darkened room

How to play: Place the baby in a carrier or infant seat about a foot from a wall. Dim the lights. Turn on the flashlight. Stand behind the baby's seat and flash the light on the wall. Slowly move the light around on the wall. Move the flashlight so the light moves in different kinds of patterns:

- ◆ Very slowly shine the light back and forth to make a horizontal line of light.
- ◆ Very slowly move the light up and down to make a vertical line of light.
- ◆ Very slowly, move the light to form a pattern of little circles on the wall.
- ◆ Make zigzags, and see if your baby tries to follow the light with her eyes.

Finale

At one month, your baby still cannot see very clearly beyond 18 inches (46 cm). But she will study anything within range of vision. Just to entertain your baby, play classical music and use a flashlight to make patterns on the wall. Keep beat to the rhythm of the music. Move the light up and down, back and forth, or round and round.

Encore

Remember: your baby has limited ways of telling you when she has had enough stimulation. Be alert for her cues, and if she seems over-stimulated, end the game you are playing immediately.

Fling Your Foot

Kick, kick, fling your foot.
Kick the ball over the roof.

Overture

In the early months, your baby cannot see color as vividly as older children, so it is important to show him black and white objects or pictures. But he will still enjoy a colorful mobile hung over his crib. Hang a mobile over your baby's crib and observe him watching it. During the days to come, he will begin to register color. When he has mastered more motor control, he will begin to kick and reach toward the objects on the mobile as they move around.

Performance

Play: To encourage your baby to kick purposefully, play "Fling Your Foot."
What you will need: Beach ball, duct tape, elastic
How to play: Lay the baby on the floor. Use duct tape to fasten the elastic to the ball. Tape the other end of the elastic to the ceiling, then suspend the beach ball over the baby within reach of his hands and feet. Make sure the ball will bounce up and down and sway from side to side. Show your baby how to use his hands and feet to move the ball. With great fanfare, each time he causes the ball to move, verbally praise your baby. Bat the ball around so it moves over your baby. See if he moves his eyes and head to follow the ball.

Finale

Use a variety of things suspended from the ceiling with elastic to stimulate baby to move feet and hands in directed play including:

- Transparent scarf
- Rag doll or teddy bear
- Wind chimes
- Bell
- Musical mobile

Encore

To encourage your baby to move his arms and hands in a purposeful way, entertain him with common materials:

- Pinwheels—Blow to spin a pinwheel in front of him.
- Streamers—Wave streamers around him
- Scarves—Wave a translucent scarf around him
- Tins—Individual pie-sized aluminum tins
- Puppets—Paper plate puppets (Draw simple features on a plate with black marker.)

 © Instructional Fair • TS Denison

Keeping Track

Milestone	Date	Comments
Comforted by rocking and singing		
Comforted by sucking pacifier or thumb		
May have a fussy time late in the afternoon		
Comforted by cuddling and swaddling		
Gives you the first smile		
Recognizes Mother's voice and a few others		
Begins to make sounds		
Moves his/her eyes around in all directions		
Able to follow an object with his/her eyes		
Notices and watches his/her own hands and feet		
Responds to a rattle shaken within his/her vision		
Begins to be able to control his/her head		
Begins to kick and grab purposefully		

Big Changes

Playing with Your Two- to Three-Month-Old

Contemplate

Last month your infant began to show signs of recognizing you; she probably gave you her first big smiles; more than likely you heard her first giggles. You saw little changes that made communicating with your baby possible. In the next two months you will see big changes. Your baby will want desperately to communicate with you. She will make sounds, faces, and show affection.

The changes that you see happening over the next two months will be great ones. What she cannot do today, within the next day or week she will be accomplishing with flare. If you attempt a game and it is just too advanced for your baby, wait a day or a week; then try it again. In fact, repeat the activities in this chapter several times during the next two months. Make notes on her alertness and abilities. Then reread your notes a month later when you play the same game again. The developmental accomplishments in this period will be tremendous and fun to watch.

Milestones: Two- to Three-Months-Old

- ◆ Will be able to grasp and hold a rattle
- ◆ Will like gazing at his own hands
- ◆ Will babble and imitate sounds she hears
- ◆ Will be able to support his own head
- ◆ Will become interested in gazing into a mirror
- ◆ Will prefer sweet smells and flavors
- ◆ Her hearing will become fully matured
- ◆ Will still prefer the human face to all other patterns
- ◆ Will respond to a smile with a smile
- ◆ Will be able to focus on things 8–10 inches (20–24 cm) away
- ◆ Will open and close his hand and grasp objects in view
- ◆ Will bat at dangling objects with hands
- ◆ Will stretch legs out and kick when lying on stomach or back

 © Instructional Fair • TS Denison

 ### General Tips

The two- and three-month-old child learns by watching. Observe closely, and you might catch her glances lingering when an object she wants disappears from her sight. She will also spend a lot of time watching her own hands and will look at objects when placed in her line of vision. She will begin to like looking at objects in primary colors because she is now able to distinguish between colors. By the end of this period, she will most likely be able to follow a slow-moving, bright object for several minutes.

Her grasp is not yet good enough to allow her to hold objects and explore them. But her fine motor skill of grasping a finger will now include holding a rattle when it is placed in her hand. She will reach for dangling objects and will still grasp your finger when you put it in her hand.

Your baby will still be startled when touched unexpectedly, so let her know when you are approaching by speaking in a soft voice. She will begin to enjoy water and probably like her bath. She will respond to stimuli with her whole body. For example, when in a warm bath, she will splash the water with her hands and feet. Although her head still needs support, when placed on her stomach, she will be able to lift her head. Hold her up with feet touching the floor, and she will be able to bear some of her own weight.

Her language of crying will become even more sophisticated. She will use variations in tone and intensity when crying to express different needs. Auditory skills will include recognizing her mother's voice and the voices of other familiar people. At this age, her favorite sound to hear is the human voice. She will smile, coo, chuckle, and gurgle as if having a conversation with familiar faces. She will even be able to vocalize similar sounds when her own sounds are repeated.

Appropriate toys for the two- and three-month-old child include:
- Hand puppet with simple features
- Books with high-contrast patterns in black and white
- Board books with simple, colorful pictures of familiar objects
- Bright, varied mobile hung over the crib
- Unbreakable mirror attached to the side of the crib
- Rattles
- Music boxes
- CDs to be played: lullabies, classical music, children's songs

Playing with Your **Two- to Three-Month-Old**

Rattle, Rattle

But when he meant to quail and shake the orb,
He was as rattling thunder.
—William Shakespeare

Overture

In the first two months your baby explored his environment with his eyes and ears only. But now he will begin to reach out with his hands as well.

Performance

Play: To give your baby practice holding a rattle and shaking it, play "Rattle, Rattle."
What you will need: Baby rattles
How to play: Sit the baby in a carrier or infant seat. Shake a rattle about a 12 inches (31 cm) from his face. Offer it to him. Help him learn how to hold it. Say, "Rattle, rattle." Show him how to move his hand to rattle it. Try a rattle in each hand. Say, "Rattle, rattle."

Finale

During the first two months your baby was a helpless creature. Now that he can reach out and explore his environment a bit, he will be highly motivated to touch and feel objects. When you see him trying to grab something, if it is appropriate, hold it in front of him so he can explore it with his eyes and fingers. Safe things in the house for him to touch and feel include:

◆ Sheets of aluminum foil, paper, or waxed paper to crumple
◆ Small cardboard boxes
◆ Plastic hand mirror
◆ Small, soft stuffed animals
◆ New, hard-rubber pet toys with bells inside
◆ Swatches of materials such as burlap, velvet, silk, corduroy, wool, satin, and cotton
◆ Foam rubber balls
◆ New sponges, all sizes and colors
◆ Cloth blocks
◆ Variety of homemade mobiles

Encore

Cradle gyms or bars that go across the width of a crib will offer your baby good educational exploration. Touching and viewing a cradle gym will advance your baby's eye-hand coordination and stimulate him. Make sure you select a cradle gym that has an assortment of simple objects that your baby can touch or strike. There are different brands available. Choose one that will provide a variety of experiences because in the months to come your baby will learn how to hold and manipulate things with his hands.

        © Instructional Fair • TS Denison

Clap Your Hands

> *Do you believe in fairies?. . .*
> *If you believe, clap your hands!*
> —Sir James Matthew Barrie

Overture

Watch your baby, and you will see that one of the most fascinating things to her is her own hands. Most babies this age spend hours just watching their own hands.

Performance

Play: To give your baby an opportunity to entertain herself with her hands, play "Clap Your Hands."

What you will need: No special equipment is needed to play this game.

How to play: Clap your hands, and let your baby discover that when they touch, they make a sound. Clap softly. Clap loudly. Clap slowly. Clap quickly. Hold your baby's hands in yours, and clap them together. Show your baby that when her hands come together they make a clapping sound. Guide her clapping softly, slowly, and quickly. Tell your baby what a good clapper she is. Applaud when you see her learning new things.

Finale

Encourage the action of bringing hands together by putting a rattle in each of her hands. Show her how to shake the rattles by bringing them together with a bang. If your baby cannot grasp a rattle in both hands at once, wait a week or month to try this activity.

Encore

Hand-eye coordination can also be reinforced by having your baby try to touch something that you put in front of her. Make a game of it. Use a small stuffed toy that she can grasp. Touch it to her nose, then hold it out in front of her face and ask, "Can you touch this?" Move it around to stimulate her desire to touch it. When she reaches for it, move it slightly from side to side. Every few seconds, let her try to hold it. When she drops it, pick it up and begin the game again. Trying to touch it will give your baby good eye-hand coordination practice. But do not frustrate her with this game. If she cries or does not like it when you move the toy away, do not play this game until she is older. If she cannot yet hold it, play this game again in a few weeks when she will be able to grasp it.

Babble, Babble

Babble, babble, babies babble.
Dabble, dabble, mommies dabble.

Overture

Watch and listen, and you will see that your baby enjoys making sounds. He will use humming, cooing, and babbling to make all kinds of noises to entertain himself. He may even experiment with his cries, lowering and raising the pitch, pausing to see if he can hear you coming, etc. Babies this age can mimic some of the sounds they hear others make.

Performance

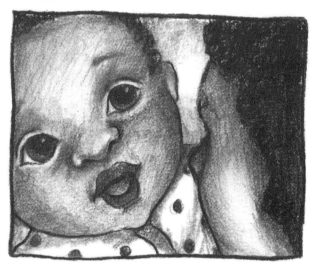

Play: Give your baby an opportunity to communicate with you by playing "Babble, babble."
What you will need: No special equipment is needed to play this game.
How to play: Place your baby in your lap so he can see your mouth. Listen for the sounds he makes and mimic them. If he coos—you coo. If he babbles—you babble. Whatever sounds he makes, try to duplicate them. Repeat each of his sounds several times as if having a conversation.

Finale

Hearing your speech gives your baby a head start in oral language development, which is the foundation for later written language and reading. Make a list of the sounds your baby makes. See if you can connect the sounds with particular occasions (like bath time or feeding) or with an object (sibling, family pet, or toy). Use his sounds like words to converse during the day. If baby says "Goo, goo, gaga" when he sees the family pet, use the same sounds when you talk about the pet. Talk to him about things using his "words." Your babbling conversations will teach him communication rules: taking turns, vocal tones, imitation, and pacing of sounds.

Encore

Long before your baby understands or repeats any specific words, he will be interested in listening to you and others talk to him. It is important to establish rapport with your baby. Intellectual stimulation in infancy will go far in increasing your baby's understanding of the world. An early grasp of language will depend upon the words he hears used in your home. Talk to your baby in "baby talk," as well as at times use appropriate terms and a varied vocabulary.

© Instructional Fair • TS Denison

Up We Go!

Up, up, up we go.
Hold on tight. Don't let go.

Overture

Holding your baby by her hands, slowly lift her to an upright position. Watch when you carefully pull her up by her hands; her head will lag. Her neck muscles are not yet strong enough to hold her head erect.

Performance

Play: To encourage your baby to strengthen her grasp (hold) and exercise her neck and arm muscles, play "Up We Go."

What you will need: No special equipment is needed to play this game.

How to play: Place your baby on the floor and give her both of your index fingers to grasp in her hands. (Hold her hands if your baby is not strong enough to grasp your fingers.) Slowly pull her up to a sitting position, and then slowly lay her back down. Repeat three or four times. Use your smiles to reassure your baby that her grasp is strong enough to hold her. When she depends upon her own grasp, she is learning to trust her own strength.

Finale

When you let your baby grab your fingers, you are helping her strengthen her wrist, arm, and upper body. Squeezing is good exercise for her. Exercise her grasping grip by giving her your index finger to squeeze. Then remove it from her grasp and give her another finger to grasp. Alternate all ten fingers and thumbs several times.

Encore

Other ways to exercise her grasp hold include:

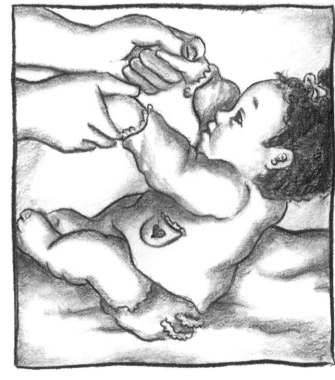

- ◆ Have her grasp something, such as a rattle, tug it gently and try to pull it from her grasp.
- ◆ Grasp her hands in yours as she is grasping back. Lift her from an upright position to several inches from the floor. Carefully lower her again.
- ◆ Have her grasp your index fingers in her hands. Then gently try to pull your fingers from her grasp.
- ◆ When you grasp your baby's hands say "I love you." Then each time you grasp her hands she will hear an unspoken "I love you."

Mirror, Mirror

Mirror, Mirror, on the wall,
Who's the fairest of them all?
—Snow White

Overture

At two to three months your baby will begin to show an interest in mirrors. Watch him when he catches a glance of himself in a mirror.

Performance

Play: To stimulate your baby's visual interest, play "Mirror, Mirror."
What you will need: Steel mirrors about 4 or 5 inches (10 or 13 cm) in diameter
How to play: Place your baby in a carrier or infant seat. Use a mirror held about 10 inches (25 cm) from his face so he can see his own image. Talk to him about how beautiful he is. Show him your image in the mirror. Wave to your baby in the mirror. Call your baby's image in the mirror by your baby's name. Say something like: "There is (baby's name) in the mirror. You have a beautiful face, (baby's name)." Let baby help you hold the mirror. Look at the reflection of other objects in the mirror:

- Hold up a stuffed animal so your baby can see the image of the animal in the mirror.
- Hold up a toy so your baby can see the image of the toy in the mirror.

Finale

Although a baby enjoys looking at his own face, the faces he prefers to gaze at are his mother's and father's. To make sure your baby has plenty of time to look at you:

- Smile and make faces at him while you hold and feed him.
- Put your face close to his and talk to him during the day.
- When he wakes up in the morning or after a nap, greet him by gazing into his eyes for awhile.
- Display large photographs of Mother and Father in the baby's room.
- Use faces of people cut from magazines to decorate the wall near his crib.

Encore

Two-sided baby mirrors framed with finger-sized holes for easy grasping are available at most toy stores. Hang one on the side of his crib. Later it will be just right for him to carry around with him. Use a variety of mirror play to stimulate your baby including:

- Place him on the floor in front of a full-length mirror.
- Sit him in a carrier or infant seat where he can see himself in a mirror.
- Put a mirror on the wall in his room.
- Show him how he looks in the bathroom mirror.
- Stop to let him look in tri-fold mirrors in department stores.

© Instructional Fair • TS Denison

Sniff, Sniff

Polly put the kettle on,
Polly put the kettle on,
Polly put the kettle on,
And let's drink tea.
　　　　　—Traditional Rhyme

Overture

Watch, and you will see how your baby explores the world with her mouth. Everything she can pick up will go into her mouth. Right now her mouth is her most important sensory organ. Later, she will be more stimulated by sights and sounds, but for now she is forming mental models of objects in her brain and learning about her environment by using her mouth.

Performance

Play: To help your baby experience a variety of sweet smells, play "Sniff, Sniff."
What you will need: Fruit cut into large wedges: apple, banana, orange, peach
How to play: Put your baby in a carrier or infant seat. Place the wedges of fruit on a plate. Carefully hold a wedge of fruit near the baby's nose so she can experience the aroma. Tell her, "Sniff, sniff." As she experiences the smell of the apple, name it—"apple." Do the same with the other fruits.

Finale

Use your baby's sense of smell to stimulate her. Put foods with pleasant aromas in plastic containers with tight-fitting lids. Examples: mashed banana, apple sauce, chocolate chips, etc. Poke holes in the lids. Hold each container near your baby's nose and squeeze it so the aroma leaves the container. Name each aroma for your baby. Watch to see which smells are her favorites. On different days, experiment with cotton balls with a drop of Mother's favorite perfume, vanilla, peppermint extract, and Father's aftershave lotion. Each time your baby sniffs an aroma, name the aroma for her.

Encore

Because your baby likes to put things into her mouth, as soon as she learns to grasp and hold things, you will need to be extra cautious about what she can reach. Some parents let their babies play with inflated balloons. Because a balloon can pop and then be swallowed, we do not recommend balloon play for babies. Other things with which to avoid letting your baby play include:
- Anything smaller than a table tennis ball
- Anything that has tiny pieces that can be broken off and swallowed
- Anything sharp like a drinking straw that can poke the skin or eyes
- Anything glass that can break and cut
- Anything with sharp edges that can cut
- Thin sheets of paper that can cut skin or lips
- Anything with sharp corners

Shhh, Listen

Shhh, listen, be quiet as a mouse.
Shhh, listen, someone's in the house?

Overture

Watch your baby, and you may see him becoming still when he is listening to something he wants to hear. By three months, your baby's hearing will be fully matured. At this age, his favorite sound is that of familiar human voices.

Performance

Play: To reinforce your baby's listening, play "Shhh, Listen."
What you will need: Rattle and small bell
How to play: Place your baby in a carrier or an infant seat. Place the rattle and bell on the floor between you and your baby. Tell him "Shhh, listen." Shake the rattle and then place it on the floor. Repeat with the bell. Each time you are going to use one of the noisemakers, tell your baby, "Shhh, listen." By your example, you can teach him "Shhhh" means to be very quiet. Try using one of the noisemakers behind your baby where he cannot see it. Then show him which one you used. Name it each time he hears its sound.

Finale

Use a variety of noisemakers to play the "Shhh, Listen" game including:
- Drum
- Horn
- Clinking ice in a glass
- Crumpling cellophane
- Sandpaper blocks
- Whistle

When your baby is quiet, use a noisemaker. Then name the noisemaker for him. If it is appropriate, let him touch each one.

Encore

To provide your baby with an opportunity to hear a variety of sounds, take him on a listening walk. Stroll him in a park or mall and tell him, "Shhh, listen." Then show him by your posture and stillness that you are listening. Name the sounds you hear. Try to expose him to a variety of nature sounds including:
- Rustling leaves
- Birds singing
- Dog barking
- Rain spattering on the sidewalk
- Wind blowing
- Dried leaves crunching underfoot
- Waves crashing on the beach
- Sounds that animals make in a zoo, pet store, or on an farm

© Instructional Fair • TS Denison

Making Faces

Laughing eyes, smiling lips,
I see joy in your face.

Overture

Although your baby may still have trouble focusing her eyes and is just beginning to see color, she is capable of seeing much more than you may think she can. Everything she sees, hears, and feels is being stored in her brain. Right now your baby prefers the human face to all other patterns.

Performance

Play: To entertain your baby with faces, play "Making Faces."

What you will need: No special equipment is needed to play this game.

How to play: Seat your baby in a carrier or an infant seat. Make a face. Try naming your facial expressions so you can verbalize about them.

Examples:

- ◆ Prune face—Scrunch up face like a prune.
- ◆ Sour face—Grimace like eating a lemon.
- ◆ Happy face—Smile your biggest smile.
- ◆ Pouting face—Make a pout.
- ◆ Clown face—Cross eyes, stick out tongue, and look silly.

Finale

Because your baby is highly motivated by faces, she will enjoy seeing faces of people. Cut large, colorful pictures of people from magazines. Mount them on cardboard and place them around your baby's crib where she can see them or prop the pictures near the baby when she is resting on a blanket on the floor. Faces of children will especially be interesting to her. Include pictures of people of different cultures.

Encore

Tell your baby what you like about her face. Name the color of her eyes, hair, and skin. Describe her nose and lips. Tell her which of her features she shares with family members. Touch her face gently and lovingly. Trace her smile with your index finger. Pat her cheeks. Gently squeeze her nose. Touch each part of her face and tell her how much you like each feature.

I See a Smile

The smile on your face lets me know—
There's a song in your heart.

Overture

Watch, and you will see that by three months your baby will be a master of "smile talk." He will quickly learn that by smiling he can get the attention of those around him. He will watch your face until you give him a smile, then he will beam one right back to you.

Performance

Play: To encourage your baby to respond to a smile with a smile, play "I See a Smile."
What you will need: No special equipment is needed to play this game.
How to play: Every time you see your baby smile tell him, "I see a smile!" Then sometimes when he is sad or crying you can trigger a smile by saying, "I see a smile." Then look at him, and wait for his sadness to fade and his mouth to turn upward into a smile.

Finale

Smiling is a natural phenomenon brought on by pleasant thoughts or stimuli. Use your baby's smiles to get an idea of what brings him the most pleasure. Stimulate his senses in a variety of ways, and note which of his senses brings the most and biggest smiles to his face.

- ◆ Listening—Play classical music for him; sing to him; coo at him.
- ◆ Touching—Give him a back rub; bathe him in warm, bubbly water; give him hugs and kisses.
- ◆ Taste—Let him taste tapioca pudding, apple sauce, vanilla ice cream.
- ◆ Viewing—Show him a variety of big pictures of animals; take him to a pet store; or give him a tiny, stuffed animal with which to play.
- ◆ Smelling—Let him smell chocolate chip cookies baking in the oven; put a little perfume on his sleeve; let him smell aromatic flowers.

Encore

Your smile means a lot to your baby. You cannot always wear a smile nor do you need to. But when you are happy, you can tell your baby about the happiness he gives you by smiling at him. You are the center of his universe. He is constantly looking to you to make sure the world is an okay place. Your smile tells your baby that all is well with the world.

© Instructional Fair • TS Denison

Watch the Birdie

For some must watch, while some must sleep:
So runs the world away.
—William Shakespeare

Overture ....

Observe your baby, and you will see her favorite pastime is watching people. Your baby knows that other people bring her comfort and joy. She will begin to be able to focus on things out of the 18-inch (46-cm) range. She is learning to follow you with her eyes as you walk around the room.

Performance ....

Play: To help your baby practice focusing on things 18 inches (46 cm) away, play "Watch the Birdie."

What you will need: A toy bird, or big feather, or puppet of any kind

How to play: Seat your baby in a carrier or an infant seat. Place the object 18 inches (46 cm) in front of her. Say, "Watch the (name of object)." Move it slowly to the right. Then bring it back to the center. Repeat by saying, "Watch the (name of object)." Move it slowly to the left, then bring it back to the center. Say, "Watch the (name of object)" and move it up and down. Observe her eyes following the object. Does she move her head? How far out of the 18-inch (46-cm) range can she focus on an object?

Finale ....

When reinforcing your baby's ability to focus, use various objects to stimulate her senses including:
- ◆ Shimmering strips of ribbon attached to a paper drinking straw
- ◆ Sock puppet with simple dark features
- ◆ Rattling aluminum foil pie tins
- ◆ Snapping your finger and thumb
- ◆ Ringing a small bell
- ◆ Soft, musical toy

Rhythm sets designed for babies can help teach your baby to focus. Shake or rattle a tambourine with one or both hands. Purchase a chubby maraca that will be just right for very small hands when she learns to grasp.

Encore ....

On other occasions, direct your baby's attention to things out of her range of sight. When someone enters the room, direct her focus by saying, "Look, Daddy is home." Name familiar objects and point to them. Say, "Look at the (name of object)." When you are taking the baby for a ride in her stroller, point out nearby objects like trees, flowers, people, or animals.

© Instructional Fair • TS Denison

Busy Beeline

Busy as a bee,
Happy you and me.

Overture..

After a few weeks, a baby begins to be aware of the direct effect his own actions have on the physical world. This ability to control some of his environment is the beginning of his capability to amuse himself. As he gets older, his needs will decrease, and he will be able to entertain himself for longer stretches.

Performance...

Play: To reinforce your baby's self-entertainment, create a "Busy Beeline" for him.
What you will need: A scarf, interesting things to tie to the scarf: plastic mirror, rattles, bells, toy tambourine, soft stuffed toys
How to play: Hang a scarf with interesting objects safety-pinned to it where your baby can reach it. You might hang it in front of him where he can reach it from his infant seat; you might hang it over his crib where he can reach it while resting on his back; or you might place it on the floor in front of him while he is on his tummy. To keep the play interesting, change the things on the "Busy Beeline" at least once a week.

Finale..

Encourage your baby to entertain himself by giving him interesting things to touch, hear, and see. Make a collage on a large poster board by gluing pictures from magazines in random order. Place the collage where your baby can see it. Add new pictures to the poster board, overlapping as you add new ones. Include pictures of simple, familiar objects. Or make a collage with a theme like flowers (clip pictures from a seed catalog or garden magazine), sports heroes (clip pictures from sports magazines), or animals. Consider making a collage of photographs of family members so your baby will become familiar with faces he does not get to see every day. If you will be spending holidays with family members that your baby rarely sees, show him photographs of the folks who will be there. Point to each face and name the person. Getting to know the faces before he meets the family may make it a more pleasant experience for him.

Encore...

Show your baby a book called *Big Book of Beautiful Babies* by David Ellwand (Dutton Books, 1996). The 28-page book has black and white photographs of babies. (This book will provide many enjoyable moments for your baby.) A toy you might consider for your baby is Disney's *Babies Playtime Songs*. The auditory-stimulating book produces engaging music with a light press from a finger. Each page has the words to a popular childhood song and a scene illustrating the song.

© Instructional Fair • TS Denison

Bat the Ball

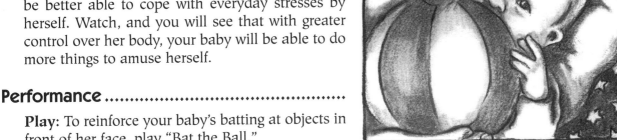

Get ready,
Get set,
Go!
      —Traditional Rhyme

Overture

As your baby's nervous system matures, she will be better able to cope with everyday stresses by herself. Watch, and you will see that with greater control over her body, your baby will be able to do more things to amuse herself.

Performance

Play: To reinforce your baby's batting at objects in front of her face, play "Bat the Ball."

What you will need: Beach ball

How to play: Place your baby in a swing, carrier, or infant seat so she is facing you. Balance a beach ball on the palm of your hand within your baby's reach. Signal your baby that she is invited to knock the ball off by saying "Bat the Ball" or giving some other verbal cue. Show your baby how to use her hand to knock the ball off of your hand. When she does, verbally congratulate her. Say something like: "Good for you, (baby's name). You batted the ball off my hand." Retrieve the ball, and repeat the exercise. Soon she will take great joy in being able to make the ball fly off your hand. Make sure you give the verbal okay for her to knock the ball off your hand by saying something like: "Get ready. Get set. Go!" You do not want to teach her to knock things out of your hand unless she is invited to do so.

Finale

Play the same game but put the ball within your baby's kicking range. Show her how to use her foot to knock the ball off your hand. Try placing the ball on her foot so that moving her foot will make the ball fall.

Encore

On other occasions, vary the object for your baby to bat out of your hand including:

- ◆ Rolled-up socks
- ◆ Paper wad
- ◆ Big feather
- ◆ Styrofoam cup
- ◆ Rattle
- ◆ Beanbag

Always use a verbal cue to invite your baby to knock an object off the palm of your hand.

Jingle Bell Mobile

Jingle bells, jingle bells,
Jingle all the way.
—"Jingle Bells"

Overture

Watch your baby, and you will see him gaining a sense of security as he begins to manipulate his environment. Having control over objects will build his self-confidence and empower him.

Performance

Play: To help strengthen your baby's legs and reinforce kicking when lying on his back, make him a jingle bell mobile.

What you will need: Varied short lengths of one-half inch (13 mm) elastic with jingle bells sewed securely to the ends and hung on a plastic coat hanger

How to play: Place the baby on his back with jingle bell mobile displayed overhead where he can reach it with his feet. Show the baby how to lift his legs and kick at the jingle bells with his feet. Say, "Kick, kick, kick." Demonstrate how the faster he kicks the more noise the bells will make. Encourage your baby to play with the bells.

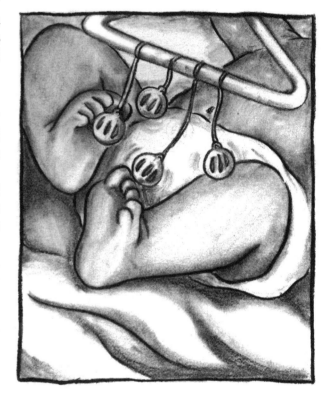

Finale

Hang the same jingle bell mobile where your baby can bat, grab, and tug on it with his hands (with adult supervision).

Encore

Stimulating your baby with musical mobiles is very important during this developmental stage. Most commercial mobiles are very cute but are not that interesting to babies. To hold your baby's attention, mobiles should be varied and changed after a few days or weeks. Create your own mobiles by hanging items from plastic coat hangers:
- ◆ Pictures of people's faces
- ◆ Things that make noise like aluminum pie pans, metal gongs, etc.
- ◆ Things that bob in a breeze like fluorescent Styrofoam balls
- ◆ Tiny metal cars
- ◆ Wads of aluminum foil of various sizes and shapes
- ◆ Basic geometric shapes cut from fluorescent cardboard (circles, squares, triangles)
- ◆ Colorful, small plastic plates, cups, and spoons

© Instructional Fair • TS Denison

Keeping Track

Milestone	Date	Comments
Can grasp and hold a rattle		
Likes to gaze at his/her own hands		
Can babble and imitate sounds heard		
Can support his/her own head		
Is interested in gazing into a mirror		
Prefers sweet smells and flavors		
Hearing is fully matured		
Prefers human faces over other patterns		
Responds to a smile		
Is able to focus on things 18 inches (46 cm) away		
Tries to grasp objects in view		
Bats at dangling objects in view		
Can stretch legs and kick at objects in view		

Sit Up and Roll Over

Playing with Your Four- to Eight-Month-Old

Contemplate

It may seem like your baby does not really know how to think and reason but she does. She cries when she wants something. She cries if she is uncomfortable and wants you to soothe her. She smiles with pleasure and enjoys watching you. But as far as having memory or an attention span, you may feel that she only reacts instead of acts. But think back about the games you have been playing with her. She may have learned a few notions by accident. When she kicked her feet to make the bells jingle, she was learning. When she batted at the beach ball and it tumbled off your hand onto the floor, she was learning. Did she remember the results of these actions from day to day? Repeating games will give you an opportunity to see how much your baby is remembering.

Things will change in the next few months. Your baby will learn that she can cause things to happen. She will remember from day to day and be able to apply learning to new situations. She will not only learn how she can affect objects, she will soon learn that she can manipulate people, too. Before long, your baby will begin intentionally dropping objects to see how they sound when they hit the floor. She will experiment to see what happens when she bats at something. She will see how far you will let her go when touching things within her reach. She will study your face to see if you are giving her nonverbal approval. During the next few months, your baby will want your approval, so disciplining will be very easy. Just a smile or frown will let her know what is expected of her.

Milestones: Four to Eight Months

- ◆ Will most likely learn how to roll from back to stomach
- ◆ Will most likely learn how to roll from stomach to back
- ◆ Will learn to sit up
- ◆ Will learn to transfer objects from one hand to the other
- ◆ Will learn to stand up (holding onto something) and support her own weight
- ◆ Will like exploring the texture of objects
- ◆ Will develop full color vision
- ◆ Will improve ability to track moving objects
- ◆ Will respond to her own name
- ◆ Will begin to understand the word "no" and names for things she sees every day
- ◆ Will discover for herself the principle called "object permanence"
- ◆ Will babble chains of consonants
- ◆ May begin trying to crawl

 © Instructional Fair • TS Denison

General Tips

At this stage of development, choosing appropriate toys for your baby is especially important. You want to stimulate your baby, but not frustrate him. Now that he will be able to grasp onto things, provide toys and objects that will encourage him to handle and explore for size, shape, color, texture, movement, position, and sound.

When introducing a new toy, do not show your baby how to play with the toy. Hand it to him. Show him how to turn it over and look at it from all sides. Then leave him to play with it in his own particular way. Odd and interesting shapes and features will be especially interesting for your baby. Objects with interesting textures will hold his interest longer than plain, smooth ones.

Often household objects will hold as much interest for your baby as will expensive toys. Things like little boxes, plastic jars filled with beans or rice, plastic measuring cups with a handle, etc., will be fun for your baby. The important thing is to vary his play with a variety of objects. As soon as your baby masters a toy, for example, playing with a rattle for a few days or weeks, he will probably discard it and not want to play with it again.

Your baby will especially like playing with toys if you are involved in the play. Talk to your baby about the toy he is holding. Name it, and describe it. Be patient when working with your baby. Your attitude toward play may well become his. And remember: his work is to play.

Appropriate toys for developing a baby's fine motor skills include:
- Unbreakable mirrors
- Baby books with board, cloth, or vinyl pages
- Magazines with pictures of people
- See-through rattles and toys so he can view what is inside
- Textured toys
- Toys that make music and sounds
- Musical instruments, such as bells, maracas, tambourine
- Soft balls

Roly-Poly Bug

Roly-poly bug
Snug in the rug.

Overture..

Learning to roll over is an unpredictable milestone. Some babies roll over as early as three months; others do not learn to roll over until after they can crawl or even walk. Your baby may be content to stay put on his back or tummy and will not care enough to roll himself over. When your baby does learn how to roll over, this first experience may be so scary that he will not attempt the move again for many days or even weeks.

Performance..

Play: Give your baby an opportunity to roll over from back to stomach, by playing "Roly-Poly Bug."
What you will need: Baby blanket
How to play: Spread out the baby blanket on a soft surface like a carpet or the grass. Put your baby in the center of the blanket on his back. Pull his little legs out straight and place arms down at his sides. Then roll him back and forth like a big rolling pin. Rock him back and forth until you finally push him over to his tummy. If he resists this movement, do not play the game. Your baby will learn to roll over in his own time.

Finale...

To give your baby the opportunity to experience the rolling motion while still feeling secure, try this exercise. Lie on your back. Put your baby on your chest. Hug him tightly to your chest with both hands and arms. Rock back and forth. Rock back and forth farther and farther until you are almost ready to roll over. At this point, let your baby slide off of you and roll over onto his back. Watch to see if your baby enjoys this exercise. If the experience is not pleasant, do not do it again. If he does enjoy the exercise, repeat several times. There is no particular time when your baby should learn to roll over. Do not try to hurry this gross motor milestone. Just play games that will show your baby what it feels like to roll over. He will learn to do it on his own when the time comes.

Encore...

Share the board book *Baby's First Year* by Debbie MacKinnon (Barrons Juveniles, 1993) with your baby. The pictures in this beautiful board book include: birth, smile, roll over, sit up, crawl, and stand. Your baby will enjoy looking at other babies doing the things he is learning to do. Another good book to share with your baby is *Baby's Day* (Baby and Toddler Board Books) by Felicity Henderson (Chariot Victor Pub., 1996). This board book also has pictures of everyday events.

 © Instructional Fair • TS Denison

Over We Go

Over the water, over the sea,
Rolling over and over,
Can you see me?

Overture

Learning to roll over will happen when your baby is ready. You cannot teach her how to roll over. However, you can help her experience the sensation to lessen its impact when she accomplishes the feat on her own.

Performance

Play: If your baby has your assistance rolling over a few times, it may not scare her when she does it on her own. Play "Over We Go."
What you will need: Blanket
How to play: Place the baby on her stomach on the edge of a blanket. Take hold of the edge of the blanket and lift it slightly so your baby will roll over onto her back. Warn her that you are going to roll her by signaling with the words "Over we go." If she enjoys the rolling game, repeat several times.

Finale

Another way to assist your baby in learning how to roll over is to lay her on her stomach. Bend one arm so her hand is at her shoulder. Bend the leg on the same side so her elbow and knee are touching. Using her hand and foot, she can easily push herself over. Gently push her shoulder until she rolls over. Taking her through these steps will help her recognize one position that makes rolling over possible.

Encore

Watch, and you may notice that your baby spends a lot of time on her back. Many babies prefer this position because it allows them an opportunity to look around at everything without holding up their heads. For a baby on her stomach, the line of vision is limited to things on one side and at eye level. Wanting to look around more is often enough motivation to get babies to roll over from stomach to back.

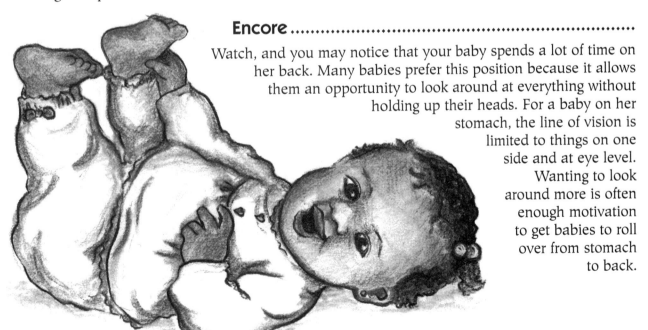

Up and Down

Here we go up, up, up.
Here we go down, down, down.
And here we go backwards and forwards.
And here we go round, round, round.
—Traditional Rhyme

Overture

In the coming months, your baby will master sitting up. In the beginning he will sit with his back rounded and head down using his arms on the floor for support.

Performance

Play: To encourage your baby to sit up, play "Up and Down."
What you will need: Soft blanket or padded quilt
How to play: Put the blanket or quilt on the floor or grass. The more padding underneath the better. Place your baby on his back and squat at his feet. Holding his hands in yours, slowly pull him to a sitting position and say "Up." Then gently lower him back down and say "Down." Each time you bring him up, give him a big smile and praise how big he is for sitting up. Practice this exercise six to ten times each day for several days.

Finale

Give your baby a chance to feel what it is like to sit up on his own. Using the soft blanket or padded quilt, place your baby on his back again. This time when you pull him up, support him at his waist. Let go of his hands so he can use them for support. Let him stay in this position for a minute or two while you talk or sing to him. Then lower him back down. Repeat this exercise three times a day for several days.

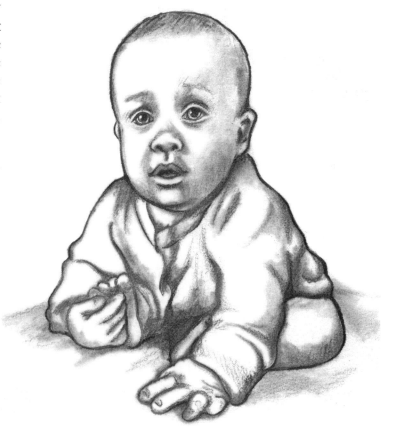

Encore

Using a particular blanket or quilt for your baby's sitting up exercises will encourage him to sit up on his own. Just place him on the blanket on his back and let him play. When he is ready, he will begin trying to sit up on his own.

 © Instructional Fair • TS Denison

Here Sits Baby

Here sits the Lord Mayor. Here sit his two men.
Here sits the cock. Here sits the hen.
Here sit the little chickens. Here they run in.
Chin chopper, chin chopper, chin chopper, chin!
—Traditional Rhyme

Overture

Watch your baby learning to sit up, and you will notice that she cannot use her hands to do anything but support herself. Learning how to do other things while sitting up will take a great deal of practice, but in time your baby will be sitting up with a strong, straight back and will not need her hands to support herself.

Performance

Play: To help your baby learn how to transfer objects from one hand to the other hand while sitting up, play "Here Sits Baby."

What you will need: Baby rattle, soft blanket or padded quilt

How to play: Place your baby on a soft blanket or padded quilt on the floor. Lay her on her back. Holding her hands in your hands, slowly bring her up to a sitting position. Using one hand on her lower back to support her, let go of both of her hands. She will automatically place her hands on the floor to help her keep balanced. Try to get her interested in a rattle. Shake the rattle to get her attention. See if she will bring one hand up to hold the rattle. If she is afraid, just let her sit up for awhile. Try the exercise every day for a week or two. Soon she will have courage to let go of the floor with one hand and grab the rattle.

Finale

Follow the same procedure as above. Place the baby on her back, on a soft blanket or padded quilt on the floor. Holding her hands in your hands, slowly bring her up to a sitting position. Using one hand on her lower back to support her, let go of both of her hands. After your baby becomes confident sitting up without using her hands for support, begin to withdraw your hand that is supporting her at the lower back. Remove it for a few seconds. Then put it back. Repeat leaving your hand off her lower back for longer and longer periods of time. When your baby is ready, play with her and hand her things to grasp. Grasping toys is a skill in itself. Her pincher grasp has not developed yet, so holding a toy will be difficult at first. Provide toys that are soft and pliable or toys with handles.

Encore

When your baby can sit up on her own, use this rhyme to play an action game.

Here sits the Lord Mayor. (*Touch Baby's forehead.*)
Here sit his two men. (*Touch Baby's eyebrows.*)
Here sits the cock. (*Touch Baby's right cheek.*)
Here sits the hen. (*Touch Baby's left cheek.*)
Here sit the little chickens. (*Touch Baby's nose.*)
Here they run in. (*Touch Baby's lips.*)
Chin chopper, chin chopper, (*Chuck Baby's chin.*)
Chin chopper, chin! (*Chuck Baby's chin again.*)

Up We Go

Up, up, up we go
Where we land, nobody knows.
—Traditional Rhyme

Overture

Watch as sometime during these next few months, your baby will learn how to stand up (holding onto something) and support his own weight. This upright position will give him a whole new view of the world. Instead of looking up at everything, he will be eye level with all the things 2 feet (61 cm) off the ground.

Performance

Play: To encourage your baby to stand up holding onto something for balance, play "Up We Go."
What you will need: A soft sofa with removable cushions
How to play: Remove the cushions from the sofa. Hold your baby's hands and say "Up we go." Stand the baby up at the sofa, and show him how to hold onto the sofa for support. Place one cushion behind the baby so that if he sits down hard his bottom will be padded. Hold his back until he gets steady legs. Let go for a second. Stay right with him, and let him get the feeling of being upright. The first time you try this, do not leave the baby to stand alone. Try this exercise several times each day for a week or two until your baby can stand alone.

Finale

Once your baby learns to grab onto things and can stand himself upright, he will be trying this exercise on his own. Make sure his crib has sides tall enough that he can stand up inside it. If he would go over the side, now is the time to try a different kind of bed. A playpen, if you use one, is a safe place for your baby to practice standing up. Place pillows in the bottom so he will have soft landings. Do not leave your baby in a playpen for longer than 20 minutes.

Encore

When your baby learns to stand up, he will enjoy having you hold his hands and help him "walk" around. Being in the upright position will be new and exciting; your baby may cry when you put him down on his back. Stand behind your baby, holding his hands up in the air and help him "walk" around.

 © Instructional Fair • TS Denison

Feelies

There was once a velveteen rabbit,
and in the beginning he was really splendid.
He was fat and bunchy, as a rabbit should be;
his coat was spotted brown and white,
he had real thread whiskers,
and his ears were lined with pink sateen.
— "The Velveteen Rabbit" by Margery Williams

Overture

Watch, and you will see that your baby spends a great deal of time exploring the texture of objects. She will spend endless moments investigating the softness, hardness, smoothness, roughness, dryness, or wetness of everything she can get her hands on. She will examine things with her hands and put them into her mouth.

Performance

Play: To give your baby a hand in her scientific research of textured objects, let her play with "Feelies."

What you will need: Eight-inch (20-cm) squares of textured fabric: velvet, satin, corduroy, burlap, flannel, and wool tweed

How to play: Wash the fabric so it will be safe for her to put the squares in her mouth. One at a time, give the fabric squares to your baby. Let her hold each one as long as she wants. On other occasions, safety pin one to the front of her clothes so she can touch, rub, and explore it.

Finale

Stuffed animals with fur, satin, velvet, flannel, and corduroy coverings will be interesting to your baby. When purchasing stuffed toys, collect a variety of different textures and colors.

Encore

Give your baby a wide variety of textures, colors, and patterns to view by choosing interesting clothing including:

- ◆ Wear interesting shirts and socks for the baby to see. Pick a few, with bright colors, lively patterns, and comfortable textured materials.
- ◆ Buy a pair of mittens and put Velcro in the palms. Attach spots of brightly colored material or fascinating textures for your baby to experience with the other hand.
- ◆ Wear interesting clothes for the baby to see. Dress up in bright colors or clothes with interesting patterns for her to view.
- ◆ Sew unusual things to the top of a shirt and wear it while holding your baby.

Looking at Books

Roses are red,
Violets are blue.

Overture

Although your baby could see at birth, he could not see things beyond a few feet or distinguish between colors. By the end of eight months, his range of vision has widened, and he is able to distinguish subtle shades of reds, blues, and yellows.

Performance

Play: To celebrate that your baby is developing full-color vision, show him brightly colored picture books.

What you will need: A book called *Baby Talk (Pudgy Board Book)* with photographs by Erika Stone (Grosset & Dunlap)

How to play: Place your baby in your lap facing out so he can see the pictures in the book. The colorful photographs of babies depict words such as:

- ◆ "Peekaboo"
- ◆ "Yum-yum"
- ◆ "Bye-bye"
- ◆ "All gone"

Look at the pictures and say the appropriate words. Use the same words during the day when your baby is performing the actions.

Finale

A good series of books for babies this age are the board books by Neil Rickien. Published by Little Simon, these books depict everyday things for baby to see.

- ◆ *Baby's Good Morning (A Super Chubby)*, 1992
- ◆ *Baby's Good Night (A Super Chubby)*, 1992
- ◆ *Baby's Neighborhood (A Super Chubby)*, 1994
- ◆ *Baby's Playtime (A Super Chubby)*, 1994

Encore

Toward the end of this developmental stage (six- to eight-months-old), introduce Kate Spohn Board Books published by Random House.

- ◆ *Piglet's Bath (Kate Spohn Board Books)*, 1998
- ◆ *Kitten's Nap (Kate Spohn Board Books)*, 1998

 © Instructional Fair • TS Denison

Yoo Hoo!

Yoo hoo, here I am.
Yoo hoo, I have bread and jam.

Overture

Watch, and you will notice that your baby can now focus her eyes on things much farther away than when she was an infant. She will begin to be aware of things happening in all parts of the room.

Performance

Play: To help your baby focus on things approximately six feet (2 m) away and improve her ability to track moving objects, play "Yoo Hoo!"

What you will need: A room with a sofa, screen, table, or other furniture that you can hide behind

How to play: Sit your baby in a carrier, an infant seat, a stroller, or swing. Place her so she can see the furniture where you will hide. She should be about six feet (2 m) away from the sofa. Go behind the sofa and yell "Yoo Hoo!" Then pop your head up where she can see you. Then go back down. Move to the other end of the sofa and say, "Yoo Hoo!" again and pop up. Repeat this game popping up at different ends of the sofa. Then use other furniture in the room to hide behind. It is okay for her to watch you hiding. She will still be delighted when you say, "Yoo Hoo!" and pop up in sight. Before you enter a room where she is, say, "Yoo Hoo!" and then pop inside the door. You will find many ways to vary the "Yoo Hoo!" game; each variation will bring giggles of delight from your four- to eight-month-old.

Finale

On other occasions, walk in front of your baby and move across the room keeping eye contact. Help her focus on you by having a conversation. Training her to use her eyes to follow you about the room will be good practice.

Encore

Stimulate your baby's focusing ability by taking her to interesting places to observe people, animals, and other objects, including:

- ◆ To a schoolyard where there are children playing. Hold her where she can see children walking and jumping
- ◆ To the park where she can see squirrels scampering around the area and climbing trees
- ◆ To a pet store or Humane Society where she can see puppies barking
- ◆ To an aquarium where she can watch colorful fish swimming
- ◆ To a zoo where she can watch monkeys climbing in cages
- ◆ To the seashore where she can watch waves crashing on the shore
- ◆ To a duck pond where she can watch ducks swimming

That's My Name

And the best and the worst of this is that neither is most to blame,
If you have forgotten my kisses, and I have forgotten your name.
—Algernon Charles Swinburne

Overture

Watch your baby when you say his name. Hearing his own name will bring a smile to his face and sparkle to his eyes. It is said that all humans like hearing the sound of their own names more than any other word.

Performance

Activity: To give your baby an opportunity to hear and respond to his name, say it often every day.
What you will need: No special equipment is needed to play this game.
How to play: Whisper your baby's name. When you see him, open your eyes wide, make eye contact, and whisper his name. Hold your hand to your heart, and let him know that the sound of his name is very special to you. Use it in games and activities. When you greet him each morning, after his nap, and before he goes to sleep, whisper his name.

Finale

When you go into his bedroom, whisper his name. Tell him that this is (baby's name)'s room. Pick up each toy and say, "This is (baby's name)'s bear," "This is (baby's name) books," etc. When you are putting on baby's clothes, tell him "This is (baby's name)'s shoes, socks, hat, coat," etc. Touch baby's face or body parts and name each one.
Examples:
- ◆ This is (baby's name)'s nose.
- ◆ These are (baby's name)'s eyes.
- ◆ This is (baby's name)'s hair.
- ◆ These are (baby's name)'s knees.

Encore

Say your baby's name many times each day. Sing it. Whisper it. Work it into your conversations as much as possible. Ask him questions like:
- ◆ "Where is (baby's name)?" Let him respond with a sound then pretend to see him for the first time. Say, "There you are! I've been looking for (baby's name)."
- ◆ When removing socks, ask, "Where is (baby's name)'s toes?" Look for them under his socks and act surprised when you find them. Say, "There are (baby's name)'s toes! I've been looking for those little toes."

   © Instructional Fair • TS Denison

Do You Know "No"?

What part of "no" do you not understand?

Overture

Watch your baby's face when you say "No," and you will know if she comprehends or not. Does your baby respond to the word "no" in an appropriate way? Because she will begin to crawl and move around on her own soon, understanding the word "no" will be important to her safety.

Performance

Play: To reinforce the meaning of the word "no," play "Do You Know 'No'?"
What you will need: Two objects, one belonging to your baby and one belonging to Mommy or Daddy
How to play: Sit the baby in a carrier or infant seat. Show her the object that belongs to her and say, "Yes, this is yours, you may touch it." Smile and hand the object to your baby. Then show her the object that does not belong to her and do not smile. Say, "No, this belongs to (name)." Do not hand it to her. Put it away. Find another object that belongs to Mommy/Daddy and show her. Do not smile. Say, "No." Then put it away. Repeat with several other things that belong to Mommy/Daddy and alternate with things that do belong to the baby that she can hold.

Finale

Babies learn language in stages. Every day she receives information about language by listening to people talk and watching how they communicate with each other. In the first few months, your baby was most concerned with tone and pitch. Now she will begin to match words with objects. Talk to her during the day. Name objects and let her hold them. Name objects and point to them. Name actions that she is performing such as: bathing, eating, drinking, sleeping, rocking, crawling, sitting, standing, etc.

Encore

The most important thing about saying "no" to your baby is to never go back on it. If you say "no" you must stick with it. Baby will learn very quickly if you give in to her crying that she can get what she wants by crying. If you are firm a few times when she is a baby and "No" means "No!" then it will be much easier raising her. Make sure you mean "no" before you say it and then NEVER go back on it!

Abracadabra

Abracadabra, now you see it.
Abracadabra, now you don't.

Overture

Watch your baby, and you will see how he is discovering for himself the principle called "object permanence." Even when he cannot see something, it still exists. In his early months he assumed that the world consisted only of things that he could see. If you left the room, he thought you no longer existed. If he dropped his rattle and could not see it, it no longer existed either.

Performance

Play: To reinforce for your baby that objects continue to exist when they are out of sight, play "Abracadabra."

What you will need: Scarf, rubber ball

How to play: Place your baby in a carrier, an infant seat, or swing sitting up. Place a rubber ball on the floor or table where he can see it. Then place the scarf over the ball. Ask him, "Where is the ball?" Then say, "Abracadabra" and with great fanfare, pull the scarf off of the ball. Say, "There it is!" Repeat several times. If you ever wanted to be a magician, now is your chance. Everything you do is magic to your baby. On other days, play the same game but hide other objects under the scarf: your baby's shoes, bottle, teddy bear, or rattle.

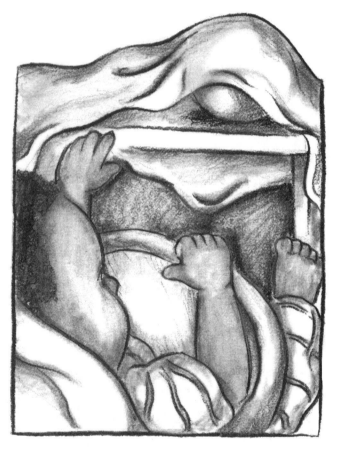

Finale

Play a varied version of peekaboo by putting the scarf over the baby's head and asking "Where is (baby's name)?" Say, "Abracadabra!" Pull off the scarf and act surprised. Then say, "There you are! Where were you?" Use the scarf to cover your own head and repeat the process.

Encore

Play other games to reinforce permanency. Show the baby a favorite toy. Then as he watches, place the toy behind your back and ask, "Where did it go?" Then say, "Abracadabra!" and bring it back in sight. When covering baby with a blanket at night, bring it over his head and say, "Where is (baby's name)?" Then say, "Abracadabra!" and pull the blanket off his head. Act very surprised and say something like this: "Where did you go? I couldn't see you?"

 © Instructional Fair • TS Denison

Buzz and Hum

Buzz, quoth the blue fly,
Hum, quoth the bee,
Buzz and hum they cry,
And so do we.
—Traditional Rhyme

Overture

Beside hearing sounds, your baby has been making her own sounds in the form of cries and coos. At about four months she will begin to babble. She will babble with rhythms and characteristics of her native language. Listen to the babble of your baby, and you will hear her raising and lowering her voice as if she is making a statement or asking a question.

Performance

Play: To encourage your baby to babble chains of consonants by playing "Buzz and Hum."
What you will need: No special equipment is needed to play this game.
How to play: Listen to the sounds your baby makes. Then echo the sounds back. Your baby may find it amusing, and she will feel like she is having a conversation with you. The more you acknowledge the sounds she makes, the more motivated she will be to use sounds to communicate.

Finale

Your baby will make lots of new sounds. Besides echoing a sound your baby makes, take it one step further. Give some examples of words that begin with that same sound.
Examples:
- Buzz—Echo "buzz," then say: "bus," "button," "bumper."
- Hum—Echo "hum," then say: "humble," "hummingbird."
- Ma—Echo "ma," then say: "mama," "mop," "moth."
- Goo goo—Echo "goo goo," then say: "good," "goose," "goofy."
- Gaga—Echo "gaga," and then say: "got" "gotcha."
- Pa—Echo "pa," and then say: "papa," "Popsicle," "popcorn."
- Ba—Echo "ba," and then say: "bottle," "box," "baa, baa, black sheep."
- Bye-bye—Echo "bye-bye," and then say "bicycle," "bite."

Encore

Always acknowledge your baby's attempt to communicate. Talk to her every day. Stop and listen and look at her when she is babbling. Tell her how wonderful all the sounds are she makes.

Sleeping Turtle

The turtle lives 'twixt plated decks
—Ogden Nash

Overture

Watch your baby trying to learn to crawl, and it may look simple. But actually, crawling is a complex skill involving coordination of the movements of many muscles. Infants are provided with varying opportunities for physical exercise and few receive specific lessons in crawling—yet most babies learn to crawl sometime between the seventh month and first birthday. If your baby is not trying to crawl by the eighth month, do not give it a second thought. It will happen at exactly the right time for your baby.

Performance

Play: To give your baby plenty of opportunity to strengthen the muscles he will need for crawling, play "Sleeping Turtle."

What you will need: No special equipment is needed to play this game.

How to play: Place your baby on his stomach on a flat surface. Watch to see if he gets up on all fours. If he does not, use your hands to pull him up at the waist so his knees and hands are on the floor. Get down on the floor on all fours. Pretend to be a turtle and tuck your head down between your arms. Draw in like a turtle in a shell. Tell your baby you are a sleeping turtle. Then fling your head up and arch your back like a turtle coming out of its shell. Now tell the baby the turtle is waking up. These are movements your baby will make on his own. But he will find it very amusing that you are on the floor doing the things he does.

Finale

Your baby will do many exercises that are getting him ready to crawl. Encourage and assist when you see him:

- ◆ Rocking on hands and knees
- ◆ Digging with knees and pushing off
- ◆ Pushing backwards and moving across the floor feet first
- ◆ Scooting along on his bottom
- ◆ Slithering like a snake

Encore

Watch your baby, and you will see that he is constantly in motion. Placed on his stomach, he will arch his neck and look around. He will move his legs in a crawling motion. Placed on his back, he will kick his limbs. All of these movements are good exercise for strengthening his crawling muscles.

© Instructional Fair • TS Denison

Keeping Track

Milestone	Date	Comments
Can roll over from back to stomach		
Can roll over from stomach to back		
Can sit up		
Can transfer objects from hand to hand		
Can stand up with support		
Can explore texture of objects		
Will develop full color vision		
Can track moving objects		
Responds to his/her own name		
Understands the word "no"		
Understands names of familiar objects		
Understands the concept of permanence		
Babbles chains of consonants		
May begin to try to crawl		

Creepy Crawly

Playing with Your Nine- to Twelve-Month-Old

Contemplate

During these next three months, your baby will become very mobile. Although it will be very exciting to see him independently moving about, it will also be an anxious time. While immobile, you could leave him playing for short periods of time and know where he was. That will no longer be true. Within a few seconds, your baby can crawl into danger. It is time to childproof your house. While it is important for your baby's intellectual development to explore, you will need to use gates and closed doors to restrict his movement into areas where he can get hurt. Put away valuables that he might accidentally break.

Because your baby will be driven to move around, everyday happenings such as feeding, sleeping, diapering, and dressing will all be different. Issues of safety, discipline, and socializing will change how things have been done previously. The dynamics on a family of a baby this age are far reaching. The motor spurts may well keep you drained of energy and short on patience. Remember, your baby is working on many new skills. At times the world will seem very frustrating for your baby.

Milestones: Nine to Twelve Months

◆ Will learn to crawl
◆ Will begin to use pincher grip
◆ Will be able to sit without support
◆ Will pull himself to a standing position while holding onto furniture
◆ Will stand momentarily without support
◆ Will be able to bang two things together
◆ Will poke at things with index finger
◆ Attention span will grow
◆ Will begin to use objects correctly including: brush, cup, spoon
◆ Will begin to finger-feed himself
◆ Will begin to explore foods with fingers and try to use eating utensils
◆ Will be able to drop something at will
◆ Will learn to extend arms and legs to help when being dressed

© Instructional Fair • TS Denison

General Tips

Babies this age enjoy playing with simple household objects. As long as an object is clean, has no sharp edges, will not break (such as glass), and will not fit into her mouth, if your baby wants to play with it, let her. Remember, her favorite toy will be you. Play with your baby as often as you can. She will enjoy any game you want to play. Watch, and you will notice your baby is good at imitating the movements and sounds that she sees.

Over the next few months she will begin to entertain herself and play for periods by herself. She will also enjoy watching you work. While cooking in the kitchen, put her in her high chair where she can see what you are doing. Talk to her and explain what you are doing. Name objects and allow her to touch things as you name them. If you are outside gardening, give her a big wooden spoon, and let her dig in the dirt, too. She will probably enjoy playing in mud, water, and sand.

When shopping for groceries, your baby will be able to sit up in the cart and watch what you are doing. Use the supermarket as a classroom. Name vegetables as you put them in bags. Show her pictures of vegetables on cans and again, name them. Everywhere you go, everything you do will be a learning experience for your baby. Remember, she is learning to label everything now so speak slowly, keep it simple, and serve it up with a smile!

You may think that you do not have time to play with your baby all day long. But play does not have to be constant. Take extra time out to be with your baby for five or ten minutes at a time, talking, singing, and cooing to her when she is being dressed, fed, changed, and bathed. This play-time is the most important thing you can do to stimulate her intellect and demonstrate social skills. The five- to ten-minute play sessions half a dozen times each day will change your baby in a positive way for the rest of her life.

Appropriate toys for developing a baby's fine motor skills include:
- Brightly colored pieces of textured cloth
- Smooth stones too big to fit into her mouth, however small enough to grasp
- Large seashells (again, too big to fit into her mouth and having no sharp edges)
- Plastic cups, pan lids, etc.
- Balls of varied sizes and textures
- New sponges in varied shapes and colors
- Specially made plastic toy rings with large keys attached
- Rattles
- Pull toys
- Busy boxes

Come and Get It

Come take up your hats, and away let us haste,
To the Butterfly's Ball, and the Grasshopper's Feast.
—Traditional Rhyme

Overture

To encourage your baby to crawl, present intriguing objects placed just beyond his reach.

Performance

Play: When you think your baby is ready to begin crawling, encourage him by playing "Come and Get It."

What you will need: Baby's favorite toy

How to play: Place your baby on the floor. Put his favorite toy just out of reach. Tell him "Come and get it." Lift him slightly off the floor with hands and knees on the floor. When he moves his legs in a crawling way, scoot him forward enough to reach the toy. Let him hold the toy for a few minutes. Then place it just out of his reach again. Repeat the command "Come and get it." Lift him and scoot him along. Show him how to crawl several times each day for a week or two.

Finale

Crawling means different things to different babies. Some babies get up on hands and knees to crawl the regular way. Other babies stand up and use their hands and feet to move like a spider across the floor. Other babies slither on their tummies like a snake. Still others pull themselves with hands and arms and let their legs drag behind them. Your baby will have his own way of crawling that suits him best. Do not try to show him a correct way to crawl or change the method that works best for him. When your baby learns to crawl, it will empower him to be mobile. Be sure to close and lock outside doors leading to swimming pools and unfenced yards. With his new mobility will come a certain amount of danger.

Encore

As your baby becomes more agile, play crawling games:

◆ Create miniature obstacle courses for him to crawl through. Use pillows and sofa cushions to build a winding path.
◆ Crawl around with him.
◆ Play crawling tag games.
◆ Play crawling racing games.
◆ On your hands and knees, head to head, mirror the movements your baby makes.
◆ Place the crawling baby in front of a full-length mirror so he can see himself making the movements.

© Instructional Fair • TS Denison

Pick Up

A good child, a good child,
As I suppose you be.
—Traditional Rhyme

Overture

Watch your baby trying to pick up things, and you will sometimes see *frustration*. Curious, but not yet having the skill of grasping, your baby will get a lot of practice using her little fingers to pinch and hands to grasp. What we adults take for granted—picking up and holding—is a complicated series of coordinated movements that require the use of a number of fine motor muscles.

Performance

Play: To give your baby an opportunity to use a pincher grip to pick up toys, play "Pick Up."

What you will need: For this game you will need a variety of small, interesting objects including stuffed animals and new sponges in varied shapes and colors. The toys should be small enough to be held between her thumb and index finger in a pincher grip, but not small enough to be placed in her mouth.

How to play: Sit your baby up on the floor facing you. Place a variety of toys in front of her. Pick up one and look at it. Show her the pincher grip by demonstrating the hold yourself. Watch to see which toy she picks up. Name and talk about the toy she is holding. Ask her to give you the toy. Then place the toy back on the floor. Watch to see which toy she picks up next. Name and talk about each toy as she picks them up. As she loses interest or her grasp on a toy, encourage her to pick up another one. Ask, "Which one do you like?" or "Which one do you want to hold?"

Finale

To encourage your baby to practice grasping with hands instead of pinching with fingers, play the same game with larger toys—toys that will fit in the palm of her hand.

Encore

Mealtime is a great time to have your baby practice the pincher grasp. Place soft foods such as hard-boiled egg slices, soft cheese cubes, and cooked pieces of fruit and vegetables on her high chair tray. With hunger as her motivation, your baby will get plenty of practice with fine motor skills and eye-hand coordination while she feeds herself. Although it is too early for your baby to use a spoon to eat, she will like holding one and banging it on her high chair tray.

Busy Box

Higgledy, piggledy, here we sit.
Picking and plucking and making things fit.
—Traditional Rhyme

Overture

Watch your baby sitting up. Although he enjoys this posture, it will make him tired. Using neck and back muscles to balance his body is a new skill for a baby this age. When helping him sit without support, make the first sitting periods short ones. As he builds up the strength in his neck and back, he will want to sit up for longer periods.

Performance

Play: To encourage your baby to sit without the aid of support, play high-interest games that require him to sit up.

What you will need: Create a busy box by placing a variety of interesting things in a small box. You might want to include: large seashells, large smooth stones, large wooden blocks, wooden beads on rope, large bells, stuffed animals, etc.

How to play: Place your baby on a soft blanket or padded quilt. Place him in a sitting position with the box of toys in front of him. Interact with him as he experiments with the toys. In the beginning, do not let him sit up for more than ten minutes at a time.

Finale

Objects in the busy box should be changed daily or at least every other day. Providing new and interesting playthings will keep your baby's interest piqued. The more varied the objects, the more motivated your baby will be to explore them. Try to include things that will reach all of his senses, such as:

◆ Things that make interesting sounds: bells, tambourine, horn
◆ Things with different textures like fabric squares
◆ Things that smell good: hankies with a drop of perfume, pillow of potpourri
◆ Things that can be crinkled, folded, and tossed: paper, waxed paper, aluminum foil

Encore

As your baby becomes proficient at sitting up without support, he will begin leaning over to pick up toys. If he wants something which is out of his reach, he will soon teach himself to roll onto his stomach and crawl or scoot to get what he wants. Then he will sit back up again so he can play with the toy. This complicated series of steps will be mastered quite quickly because he is highly motivated to move.

© Instructional Fair • TS Denison

Choo Choo Train

I think I can,
I think I can,
I think I can.
—The Little Engine that Could

Overture

Watching your baby learn to sit, crawl, and stand will be very amazing to you. However, the small motor skills she is learning are just as amazing and require as much concentration and coordination.

Performance

Play: To encourage your baby to pull herself to a standing position while holding onto furniture, play, "Choo Choo Train."
What you will need: Two wooden chairs
How to play: Place the chairs one in front of the other like two cars in a train. Stand your baby up so she can use the second chair for support. Get on your knees and "stand" at the first chair. Pretend you are a conductor of a train. Say "Chug, chug, the choo choo train goes up the hill. Chug, chug, chug." Tell the baby that she is the caboose. Make sounds and pretend the train is moving. Although these imaginary games may not make sense to you, your baby has a rich imagination—for her it is easy to imagine that two chairs are a train.

Finale

Play pretend games about other vehicles as well.

◆ Two chairs placed side by side can become seats in an airplane.
◆ A large cardboard box or sofa can become a row boat.
◆ The top of a bed can become a raft.
◆ Several chairs set up with space between them can become a school bus.
◆ An overstuffed chair can become the front seat of a car.
◆ Two cardboard boxes placed end to end can become a race car.

Encore

Engaging in imaginative play with your baby sends a clear message to her about the value of fantasy. When you pretend that something is something else, it will encourage your baby to use her imagination.

Dance with Me

He capers, he dances, he has eyes of youth,
he writes verses, he speaks holiday, he smells April and May.
—William Shakespeare

Overture

Watch your baby when you play music. If it is music he likes, he will move with the rhythm. He may not be able to keep time yet, but he will enjoy moving to the sounds he hears.

Performance

Play: To encourage your baby to begin standing momentarily without support, play, "Dance with Me."

What you will need: Music

How to play: Turn on the music. On your knees, position yourself facing the baby holding his hands so he is standing in front of you. While supporting him with your hands, move to the music. Try twisting motions from the shoulders, up and down bopping at the waist, and moving hands back and forth in opposite directions. After a few seconds, drop one of baby's hands. Can he still stay standing? Practice with one hand for a few days until he has mastered this. On other occasions, drop both hands for a second. Gradually let him stand unsupported for longer periods at a time. The bouncing of his body to the music will help him balance and take his mind off the worry of falling. Be there to catch him so he will not take a tumble or sit down too hard.

Finale

Another way to dance with the baby is to stand behind him. Hold his arms up over his head and move to the music. He will not be able to see you, so letting go of his hands may feel a bit more risky to him. Try this varied version of dancing with your baby for brief moments on consecutive days. Try this dance in front of a full-length mirror.

Encore

If your baby seems overly concerned with his balance and does not like playing games where you control how long he must balance himself, place him in front of a soft sofa or beside a low bed where he can stand, hold on and let go at will. Try it with and without music.

 © Instructional Fair • TS Denison

Cymbals

I have become as sounding brass, or a tinkling cymbal.
—Paul the Apostle

Overture......................................

Watch your baby, and you will see how much she enjoys making sounds. Banging things together, although it may seem simple, takes a great deal of eye-hand coordination.

Performance......................................

Play: To help your baby practice banging two things together, play with cymbals.

What you will need: Two small, flat pot lids with handles

How to play: Show your baby how to hold the lids by the handles and bang them together. Use your hands over her hands to show her the movement. When you hold your baby's hands in your hands and perform a motor skill, it imprints the action in her brain. Doing something several times this way creates a path in the brain that makes the returning to that action easier for the child.

Finale......................................

Look around the house, and you will find many objects that when paired will create good "cymbals" including:

◆ Two plastic cups with handles
◆ Two large wooden spoons
◆ Two blocks of wood
◆ Two plastic dog toys with bells inside
◆ Two rattles
◆ Two cardboard gift wrap tubes

Encore ....

Providing a wide range of activities where your baby can experience success will help her develop a positive self-image. By the ninth month, babies have formed opinions regarding their own capabilities. When your baby does something, she does not know if it is good. She will look to you for your approval. If you tell her she is good and that her accomplishments are extraordinary, she will grow filled with self-worth. Take every opportunity to praise her accomplishments. When she bangs two things together, tell her she makes beautiful sounds. When she stands alone, tell her how strong she is growing. When she can sit and play by herself, tell her how proud you are of her.

Poke 'n' Poke

Although the room grows chilly,
I haven't the heart to poke poor Billy.
—Traditional Rhyme

Overture

Watch your baby exploring something new. How he tackles the task will vary depending upon his unique thoughts regarding the world. Have you ever watch youngsters poolside? Some run head-long and jump, splashing and squealing and enjoying every second of the transition from warm and dry to cold and wet. Others will gingerly walk to the edge and stick one toe into the pool to see if it is cold. Can you make any predictions about your baby and how he will behave the first time he goes swimming? Look and you will see signs of his true nature beginning to show as he tests his world.

Performance

Play: To encourage your baby to poke at things with an index finger, make a "Poke 'n' Poke."
What you will need: Sandwich-sized resealable freezer bag, jar of petroleum jelly, glitter, and glittery confetti in star shapes, duct tape
How to play: Half-fill the plastic bag with petroleum jelly, glitter, and glittery confetti. Zip the bag shut. Secure the opening with duct tape so your baby cannot open the bag. Use a finger to move the glitter and confetti around in the bag. Show your baby how to poke the bag with an index finger. Tell him, "Poke 'n' poke."

Finale

Use sandwich-sized resealable bags to make other interesting bags to poke. Try half-filling bags with any of the following and duct tape to secure the openings:

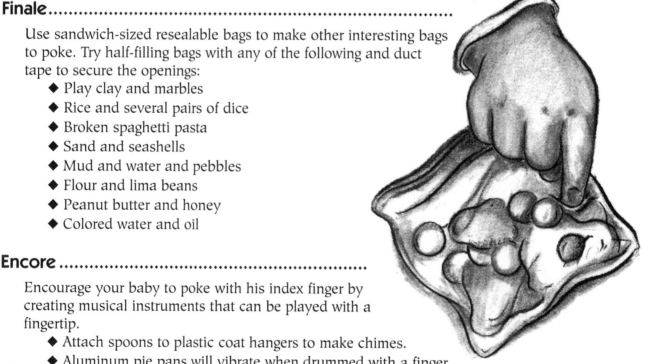

- ◆ Play clay and marbles
- ◆ Rice and several pairs of dice
- ◆ Broken spaghetti pasta
- ◆ Sand and seashells
- ◆ Mud and water and pebbles
- ◆ Flour and lima beans
- ◆ Peanut butter and honey
- ◆ Colored water and oil

Encore

Encourage your baby to poke with his index finger by creating musical instruments that can be played with a fingertip.

- ◆ Attach spoons to plastic coat hangers to make chimes.
- ◆ Aluminum pie pans will vibrate when drummed with a finger.
- ◆ Drums can be created with round food containers that are covered with aluminum foil.

 © Instructional Fair • TS Denison

I'm Proud of You

I'm proud of you. I'm proud of you.
I hope that you are proud of you, too.
—Fred Rogers

Overture

Watch, and you will notice that your baby's solitary play will last longer and longer.

Performance

Play: To help your baby lengthen her attention span, praise her when she plays alone for periods of time longer than ten minutes.

What you will need: No special equipment is needed for this game.

How to play: Each time your baby spends expended time playing alone, pick her up and praise her for being independent. Tell her something like "I'm proud of you. I like the way you can play by yourself." Rotating her toys and presenting new things for play will motivate her to play alone for longer periods of time.

Finale

As your baby develops a growing sense of herself as an individual, she will become painfully aware that you are a separate person. At first her self-awareness might produce some anxiety. Using a mirror to see herself separate from you is the beginning of this understanding of the two of you as separate people. Play, "Mirror Amusement." Sit your baby in front of a full-length mirror with a box of toys. This activity will be interesting for your baby. She will enjoy watching herself with the toys. She will pick up something and look at it and then watch her reflection in the mirror.

Encore

Because your baby is mobile now, you may not leave her alone unless she is in a safe place like a playpen. Although playpens are restrictive and should not be used for extended periods, for short ten or fifteen minute stints they will provide your baby a safe environment for play. If, for example, you have to clean a bathroom, place your baby in a playpen with toys to keep her busy. Sing or talk to her from the other room so she knows you are near. When you finish the task, take her out of the playpen right away. Praise her for playing alone. Tell her how proud you are that she can entertain herself. Making independence a positive value for your baby will help her grow to be a child and later an adult who can meet her own needs.

Play Day

Play, play every day.
—Traditional Rhyme

Overture

Watch your baby and as he learns to grasp things he will try to use them in the appropriate ways. For example, give him his hairbrush and he may use it to brush his hair.

Performance

Play: To begin playing with self-care objects in the appropriate ways, play "Play Day."
What you will need: Baby's brush, cup, spoon, book
How to play: Sit your baby on the floor. Place the four objects on the floor between you and your baby. Pick up the brush and brush his hair. Hand him the brush. Pick up the cup and pretend to drink. Hand him the cup. If your baby pretends to use the object in the appropriate way, say something like this: "Good, you are brushing your hair with the brush. Big boy!" Play with the objects one at a time in random order. Each time demonstrate its purpose and hand it to your baby.

Finale

On other occasions, use three or four items of clothing to see if your baby understands their purposes. Put them on yourself or your baby depending on to whom they belong. Just for fun, try putting on things that are too small for you like your baby's bonnet. Cover your baby's head with a large scarf. Here are some items to try:

- ◆ Hat, cap, or bonnet
- ◆ Coat or sweater
- ◆ Cape, scarf (around neck)
- ◆ Tie
- ◆ Shoes and socks
- ◆ Mittens
- ◆ Apron
- ◆ Vest

Encore

The most important part of any game you play with your baby is to make him feel successful. Watch for evidence of inner excitement and give him recognition for his successes.

 © Instructional Fair • TS Denison

Apple Pie, Pudding, and Pancakes

Apple pie, pudding, and pancakes,
Baby likes to eat.

Overture

Watch your baby when she begins to feed herself, and you will see that she is learning while she nourishes herself. Your baby is imitating, exploring, and learning to choose. By the time she is a year old, she should be allowed to feed herself at least part of each meal.

Performance

Play: To encourage your baby to finger-feed herself, you have to give her the opportunity. Although using a spoon will be difficult, give her one and let her try. Also provide foods that can be picked up with fingers.

What you will need: Baby's own spoon, soft chunks of healthful foods

How to play: Place food on the high-chair tray and let your baby explore it with fingers and spoon. If she seems frustrated, for example trying to eat pudding with a spoon, help her. Use your hand to guide her hand in the movements of spoon to bowl, dipping into the food, bringing the pudding to the mouth. You can imprint these movements in your baby's mind by holding her hand and guiding her through the process a few times.

Finale

There are many quick, practically-sugar-free foods you can make for your baby. Try some of these:

- No-Sugar, Two-Minute Apple Pie—Peel and core one apple. Cut into thin slices. Sprinkle with a crumbled cinnamon graham cracker. Cook in the microwave for 30 seconds or until the apple is soft. Let cool.
- No-Sugar, Two-Minute Apple Pudding—Add 2 tablespoons (30 ml) of instant oatmeal to 1 cup (237 ml) applesauce. Cook in the microwave 30 seconds, stir and cook another 15 seconds. Let cool.
- Heart-shaped, Apple Pancakes—Drop pancake batter in two small circles close together. With a spoon, pull down the bottom of both circles to make a heart-shape. When the pancake is cooked on one side, flip carefully. Serve with applesauce.

Encore

Babies this age need between 750 and 900 calories each day. More than half of that will come from breast milk, formula, or whole milk. Your baby should be drinking approximately 24 ounces (.72 L) of milk each day. You may be supplementing her diet with baby foods and soft foods such as puddings, mashed potatoes, yogurt, eggs, and tofu. Eating should be a time for interaction and learning. Communicating with family members at mealtime will be a great social experience for your baby. Include your baby in mealtime conversations. Acknowledge her as everyone else is talking and eating.

This Is the Way We Eat Our Food

This is the way we eat our food,
Eat our food, eat our food.
This is the way we eat our food,
Early in the morning.

Overture

Watch your baby when he is beginning to learn how to feed himself, and you will see him experimenting with the food. He will like dropping food over the edge of the tray to see what happens when it hits the floor. He might toss food to see where it will land. Some babies this age even use their spoons to catapult food across rooms. Food and eating utensils will become objects to shake, bang, throw, and drop. Remember, your baby is learning how things work. For him, mealtime is about much more than eating food.

Performance

Play: To give your baby an opportunity to explore food and eating utensils, play "This Is the Way We Eat Our Food."
What you will need: Bowl of food, spoon, cup with handle
How to play: Place a bowl of food, spoon, and cup on the high-chair tray. Place the baby in the chair. Sing the rhyme to the tune of "Here We Go 'Round the Mulberry Bush."

This is the way we eat our food,
Eat our food, eat our food.
This is the way we eat our food,
Early in the morning.

Demonstrate how to dip the spoon into the food and bring it to your mouth. Pretend to eat. Then give your baby the spoon and sing the song again. Guide your baby's hand as he dips the spoon and brings the food to his mouth.

Finale

Sing the rhyme while your baby is having his meals, especially if he is in the kitchen eating without other family members. Make mealtime an enjoyable time with songs, conversation, and laughter. Show your baby how proud you are of his self-feeding by smiling while he eats. Never criticize his for making a big mess. Tell him how proud you are that he is beginning to care for his own needs.

Encore

Take photographs of your baby's firsts including:
- ◆ First self-feeding experiences
- ◆ First time sitting up
- ◆ First steps
- ◆ First sliding down the stairs on tummy
- ◆ First crawling
- ◆ First time standing up
- ◆ First crawling up the stairs

Put the photographs in a scrapbook and write one word under each. Read the book to your baby.

 © Instructional Fair • TS Denison

Beanbag Drop

On the mark,
Get set,
Drop!

Overture

Watch your baby feeding herself, and you will probably see a great deal of the food landing on the floor instead of in her mouth. Tossing things off the edge of a high chair is so much fun. It will be very difficult to keep her from playing with food. But if you provide games that include dropping things other than food off the edge of the high chair, you may be able to help her distinguish between toys and food. Her desire to drop things may be satisfied by playing games and she will learn that food is not a toy—eating is not a game.

Performance

Play: To help your baby learn how to drop something at will, play "Beanbag Drop."
What you will need: Bulls-eye target painted on cardboard or drawn on sidewalk with chalk, beanbags
How to play: Place your baby in a high chair or swing. Put the target under the baby to one side. Place the beanbags on the high-chair tray. Show her how to drop the beanbags on the target. With great fanfare applaud her for hitting the target. Pick up the beanbags so she can drop them again and again.

Finale

Dropping things from her high chair will be great fun. Try more challenging marks as she gets the hang of the game and becomes more proficient at aiming.

- ◆ Drop tennis balls into a big bucket.
- ◆ Drop paper wads into a trash can.
- ◆ Drop table tennis balls into a bucket of water.
- ◆ Drop paper straws into a big basket.
- ◆ Drop clothespins into a big basket.

Encore

Your baby's desire to squash and squeeze foods between her fingers may be met by having her play with play clay, finger paints, mud, sand, water, etc. By playing with these craft materials you will help her distinguish between art and dinner.

Arms Up!

Arms and hands; fingers and thumbs.
Legs and knees; toes and feet.

Overture

Watch your baby as you dress him, and you may see him beginning to anticipate your moves. He may hold up one foot when it is time to put on his sock. He may pull his arm out of his coat when you are undressing him.

Performance

Play: To encourage your baby to cooperate when being dressed, verbalize what you need him to do to help you.

What you will need: No special equipment is needed for this activity.

How to play: While you are dressing or undressing your baby, explain how he can help you. For example, you might say something like this: "May I please have your arm?" Or, "Put your arms up straight in the air like this." Demonstrate what you want your baby to do. The old expression "a picture is worth a thousand words" is especially true for babies.

Finale

Another game to play with your baby is "Where Does It Go?" You will need some of his clothes including: hat, socks, shoes, shirt. Hold up one item of clothing and ask "Where does it go?" Then point to the appropriate place: head, feet, or chest. One at a time, hold up pieces of clothing and ask the question. Point to the place on his body where each item of clothing is worn.

Encore

The most important thing about playing with your child is to remember there is no right or wrong way to play. Encourage your baby to express himself freely and give him many occasions to experience positive feelings about himself. Learning to play is important for your baby's happiness. Give positive strokes to your baby often. Tell him you like the way he plays. Express your appreciation for his presence. Tell him how awesome his body and mind are. Spending time with your baby in play will send a clear message about your love for him. Remember, people spend time doing what they love best. Time spent playing with your baby means you love him best.

 © Instructional Fair • TS Denison

Bo-Peep Play

Little Bo-Peep has lost her sheep,
And can't tell where to find them.
Let them alone, and they'll come home,
and bring their tails behind them.
—Traditional Rhyme

Overture

An important thing to remember is to play the games you teach your baby, over and over. Babies experience a great deal of satisfaction when they know what to expect. Familiar games empower them.

Performance

Play: To review some of the things you have been teaching your baby, use the rhyme "Little Bo-Peep" and a stuffed lamb.

What you will need: Stuffed lamb toy

How to play: Anytime is a good time to use the lamb and the rhyme. Here are just a few suggestions:

- ◆ To practice crawling, place the lamb on the floor where the baby can see it. Say the rhyme so your baby will crawl over to get it.
- ◆ To practice gripping, say the rhyme while holding the stuffed lamb where the baby can reach it. When you finish the rhyme, hand the lamb to your baby and let him hold it.
- ◆ To practice sitting and playing independently, place the lamb in front of the baby so he can play with it while you sing or recite the rhyme.
- ◆ To practice releasing a grip, hand the lamb to the baby. While he is holding it, say the rhyme. When you finish the rhyme say, "There's Bo-Peep's lamb" and gently take it from the baby if he is willing.

Finale

At nap time or when putting your baby to bed, let finding the lamb become part of the ritual.

Little Bo-Peep has lost her sheep,
And can't tell where to find them.
"Where is Baby Lamb? Where is Bo-Peep's sheep?" (Carry your baby around or hold his hand as he walks around looking for the lamb.)
Let them alone, and they'll come home,
And bring their tails behind them.
"Here is Baby Lamb? Let's put it to bed with you." (Put Baby and lamb down for nap.)

Encore

Give your baby time to just have the lamb resting near him.

Keeping Track

Milestone	Date	Comments
Can crawl		
Can use fingers to grip		
Can sit without support		
Can stand holding onto furniture		
Can stand momentarily without support		
Can bang two things together		
Can use index finger to poke things		
Can sit and play independently		
Can use objects in appropriate ways		
Can finger-feed him/herself		
Is beginning to use a spoon and cup		
Drops things off an edge to see what happens		
Will extend arms and legs to help during dressing		

© Instructional Fair • TS Denison

PLAYING
With Your
Twelve- to Eighteen-Month-Old

© Instructional Fair • TS Denison

Look at Me!

Fine Motor Development

Contemplate

A birthday cake with one big candle signals a new developmental stage for your baby. He will keep doing all that he has been doing, except now he will become more and more skillful. His daily agenda will be to investigate, explore, discover! His whirlwind shifts of interest and movement may sometimes challenge you to your limits, but keep in mind, *play* is his work. He needs to do all the busy things he is doing so he can learn about his world.

He will pick up anything he can get his hands on. He will turn it over and examine it carefully. His curiosity and hands-on approach may keep you, his caregiver, busy just picking up after him. It will be impossible to monitor him constantly or even to bar off all the places where he cannot go. One thing you can do that will help tremendously is to teach him how to distinguish between the things he can touch, the things he can touch only with assistance, and the things he can never touch. The delicate balance between encouraging exploration and disciplining your baby may be frustrating at times, but the curiosity that triggers his desire to explore and experiment will make him a fun companion. See the tips for helping your toddler explore and yet remain safe on the following page.

Fine Motor Milestones: Twelve to Eighteen Months

- ◆ Will pick up and manipulate everything he can get his hands on
- ◆ Will enjoy making things happen
- ◆ Will enjoy filling and emptying containers
- ◆ Will learn how to hold something in both hands at once
- ◆ Will learn to grasp two or three cubes in one hand
- ◆ Will learn that things have a place where they belong
- ◆ Will learn how to stack a two- or three-block tower
- ◆ Will master picking up tiny things like raisins, using pincher grip
- ◆ Will learn how to take tiny things like raisins out of a tight-fitting container
- ◆ Will learn how to turn pages of a book, three or more at a time
- ◆ Will learn to use index finger to point
- ◆ Will learn how to wad paper into a ball
- ◆ Will learn to let go of something at will
- ◆ Will learn to use both hands to hold something large like a beach ball
- ◆ Will learn to open small hinged boxes

 General Tips

Encourage your toddler to explore and yet remain safe, and at the same time keep breakables safe, too. You will have to begin teaching your baby rules—help her distinguish between things she can touch, things she can touch with your assistance, and things she can never touch.

Providing things your baby can always touch will help divert her attention away from the things she cannot touch. Having certain places in each room where she may touch items will give her something to do besides getting into trouble. For example, one bottom drawer in the kitchen could have things that are safe for her to handle. Tell her that it is her drawer and she can get into it and play with the things stored there. You may also have a bottom drawer of a desk in the living room, a box inside your bedroom closet, and a tub of toys under the sink in the bathroom especially for your baby's play. Vary the things in these areas to keep her interest piqued.

When you are available to watch your one-year-old, rules about what she can touch will be different. There are times when she can touch certain things, but only when you are there to help her. For example, although you would not allow her to play with a telephone in your absence, when you are there to help her dial, she may be able to hold the receiver and talk to Grandpa. When your baby wants to touch and explore things that might break, you can teach her about "touching gently" and "holding carefully." (See activity on page 92.)

Things your baby can never touch might be boxed up and put away until your baby is older. However, things like kitchen knives, medicines, and detergents cannot simply disappear from the kitchen just because your baby could become hurt. In the cases of things that are dangerous and should never be touched, it will help to put them in special places high and inaccessible to your baby. All cleaning solutions should be removed from under the sinks and placed on high shelves. Medicines should be placed in locked cabinets. And, after all the precautions have been taken, you will still need to teach your toddler "No!"

Appropriate toys for developing fine motor skills in the first half of the second year include:
- Busy boxes
- Windup toys
- Latch boards
- Board books
- Old magazines with colorful pictures
- Sandbox with shovels, buckets, strainers, etc.
- Pull and push toys
- Small, soft dolls and teddy bears
- Little metal and plastic cars
- Toy telephone
- Large wooden beads to string

Nice

Boys and girls, come out to play,
The moon doth shine as bright as day.
—Traditional Rhyme

Overture

Watch your baby exploring new objects, and you will see that he is learning. Touching is how he relates to the world. Finding a balance between what he can touch and what he cannot touch will be important for his intellectual growth and your emotional well-being.

Performance

Play: To help your baby learn how to touch gently and hold carefully, play "Nice."
What you will need: Several sturdy objects that do not belong to your baby
How to play: Begin by having your baby sit down. Holding an object while sitting still is much safer than holding it while standing or moving. Explain that when holding things other than his own toys, he must be sitting. Hand him an object and say "Nice." Gently stroke the object. Show him how to nestle the object in his lap and hold it with both hands. Use your hands to show him how to turn the object and look at it from all angles. Repeat the word "nice" several times. Explain that this is something he can touch only if he has help and is told it is okay. After he has finished looking at it, take the object and carefully put it back where it belongs. Explain again that he is not to touch this object unless he has help from you. Then show him another object, repeating each step.

Finale

When your one-year-old wants to hold something that does not belong to him, teach him to point to it as a way of asking permission. Help him to learn to look to you for permission. If he picks up something he should not touch, take it from him and explain that it is not his to touch. Tell him he can look at it if he asks you first by pointing. Look him in the eyes and say something like this: "If you want to hold something that is not yours, you need to have permission. If you look at me and point to the object, I will know you want to hold it. Then I will help you hold it. Let's try." Then ask, "What do you want to hold?" If he points to the object, praise him. Reinforce his asking permission by letting him hold the object.

Encore

The place where touching is a big problem is in stores. Toddlers want to handle the merchandise. As soon as he can walk, he will want to cruise down aisles by himself. If your toddler is taught at home that he cannot hold everything he sees, shopping may be a bit easier. Confining your toddler to a shopping cart or stroller will help steer his interest to *looking* instead of touching. Confining him will also keep him from getting hurt on doors that swing open, fast-moving escalators, and stairs.

Lights On, Lights Off

On, off, on off;
Light, dark, light, dark.

Overture

Watch your one-year-old discovering the joy of turning a light switch on and off. For a child this age, to be able to control light pouring into a dark room is magical.

Performance

Play: To give your toddler an opportunity to make things happen, play "Lights On, Lights Off."

What you will need: No special equipment is needed to play this game.

How to play: If your child does not like going to bed at night, one way to convince her it is time to go to bed is to let her turn off the lights as you carry her through the house to her bedroom. Then after her bedtime story, let her turn off the light in her own room.

Finale

Your toddler will enjoy making other things happen, too. Carry her around and let her explore other switches including:

◆ Button to start dryer
◆ Remote control to turn the television on and off
◆ Knob to start dishwasher

Explain to her that these are things she can only touch when you are there to help her and guide her.

Encore

If your one-year-old is afraid of the dark, and many children this age are, a night-light will provide enough light to see things in her room. You may want to invest in a musical night-light that turns, projecting shadows on the wall and providing a soft lullaby. Some night-lights also come with aromatic oils that might be pleasant for your youngster. Letting her help choose her night-light will make it seem more special.

Young children love to play with light switches. For a special toy, mount a light switch on a board. Attach the board to the wall at eye level in a play area. Now your child can "turn the light off and on" whenever she is interested.

Fine Motor Development **Twelve- to Eighteen-Month-Old**

Filling Station

Peter, Peter, pumpkin-eater,
Had a wife, and couldn't keep her.
He put her in a pumpkin shell,
And there he kept her very well.
—Traditional Rhyme

Overture

Watch your baby's free play, and you will see his favorite activity will probably be centered around handling, filling, and emptying containers: baskets, toy box, trash cans, cardboard boxes, wagons, and cupboards. Any place he can reach will seem like a good place to put things and from which to take things out. Rearranging will keep him busy for hours.

Performance

Play: To encourage your baby's filling and emptying of containers, play "Filling Station."
What you will need: Plastic scoop, large bowl of bow-tie pasta, small unbreakable containers such as measuring cup, small cardboard box, basket, etc.
How to play: Show your baby how to use the scoop to fill the containers with pasta. Pour and shift the contents from one container to another. Also provide a container with a small neck so the pasta must be placed in the container one at a time and must be shaken to get the pasta out.

Finale

Since your toddler likes to fill and empty, provide interestingly shaped containers including:

- Plastic margarine containers and milk jugs
- Cardboard oatmeal boxes
- Large resealable bags (can be closed after filling)
- Old purses
- Toy shopping carts and wagons
- Baskets
- Plastic trash cans
- Sturdy grocery bags

Also provide objects to put in the containers:
- Tub of sand
- Tub of water
- Dried beans or pasta
- Paper and aluminum foil wads
- Styrofoam packing "peanuts"
- Natural objects like feathers, seashells, and rocks

Encore

One-year-olds also like to help with unloading jobs, such as taking dishes out of a dishwasher, clothes from a dryer, books off a shelf, food from a refrigerator, cookies out of a box and placing them in a cookie jar, and toys out of a toy box.

           © Instructional Fair • TS Denison

Take This One, Too

Intery, mintery, cutery, corn, apple seed, and apple thorn;
Wine, brier, limber lock, three geese in a flock,
One flew east, one flew west, and one flew over the goose's nest.
—Traditional Rhyme

Overture

Watch your one-year-old, and you will see how she is mastering her ability to grasp objects. A few months ago, she could not hold something with control. Soon she will be able to coordinate her hands and hold an object in each hand at the same time. She will also be able to use her hands together to hold something too big to hold in just one hand.

Performance

Play: To encourage your baby to hold something in each hand at the same time, play "Take This One, Too."

What you will need: Three small, soft toys (small enough that each one can be grasped in one hand by your baby)

How to play: Sit on the floor facing your toddler. Hand her one toy. Then hand her a second toy. When both hands are busy holding toys, say, "Take this one, too" and hand her yet another toy. She will have to drop one toy so she has a free hand to take the new toy. Do not frustrate her by being in a hurry. If she does not understand how to let go of one toy, take it from her. Then hand her the other toy. Use the toys to reinforce the skill of holding and letting go as a game. Each time her hands are full, tell her "Take this one, too." Demonstrate how you hold two toys and put one down to take the third one.

Finale

Using both hands together to hold something large like a beach ball takes a great deal of coordination. Hand your toddler a beach ball. Show her how to place her hands on either side of the ball to secure it.

Encore

Once when Beatrice Potter was asked to what she attributed her success with the Peter Rabbit books, she said it was the size of the books. She was the first author to create tiny books that fit in small hands. Many special toys for grasping are sold for babies. Small pillow dolls and tiny soft teddy bears are nice for small hands. As adults we know how frustrating it is to tackle jobs that seem too big; inappropriate toys can aggravate toddlers the same way. To make holding objects enjoyable, toys need to be the right size and have interesting textures.

Fine Motor Development **Twelve- to Eighteen-Month-Old**

Blocks

Trip and go, heave and ho!
Up and down, to and fro.
                    —Traditional Rhyme

Overture

To find out which toys interest your toddler the most, watch your toddler playing. If your toddler is like most his age, you may discover that wooden blocks are among his favorite toys. Your toddler should have an assortment of wooden blocks. If the blocks are vivid colors and a variety of shapes, they will be even more interesting and appealing.

Performance

Play: To help your toddler learn how to grasp two blocks in one hand, play "Blocks."
What you will need: A pile of small wooden blocks
How to play: Place the blocks on the floor between you and your toddler. Hand him a block. Then hand him another. Hand him a third and fourth. See if he will hold two in each hand. If he does not seem willing to try this, demonstrate how to hold two blocks. Place two blocks in his hand at once to see if he can grasp them both at the same time. If this is difficult for your child, try using paper drinking straws. See how many he can hold in each hand at once.

Finale

Use other interesting mediums to strengthen your toddler's grasp. Make it a contest. Challenge him to see how many of something he can grasp with one hand. After each contest, with great fanfare, tell him how big and strong his hands are. Try some of these:

◆ Beans from a container
◆ Marshmallows from a bowl
◆ Paper drinking straws from a pile on the floor
◆ Pebbles from a basket
◆ Cookies from a cookie jar
◆ Mud from a puddle
◆ Sand from a sandbox

Encore

Small and medium-sized cardboard boxes make good construction toys. Secure lids on the boxes with duct tape. Build towers with the largest box on the bottom graduating to the smallest on top. Let your toddler knock them down. He will soon be building cardboard box towers.

© Instructional Fair • TS Denison

Please Put It Back

Oh, that I was where I would be,
Then would I be where I am not.
But where I am I must be,
And where I would be I cannot.
                                    —Traditional Rhyme

Overture

Watch your one-year-old and you will see that she already has a sense of order. Although she does not know where things go, she likes and feels secure knowing that adults have control and the world is not chaotic.

Performance

Play: To give your one-year-old practice putting things away, play "Please Put It Back."

What you will need: Low kitchen cupboards where plastic bowls, boxes of food, etc. are kept

How to play: Explore the kitchen with your one-year-old. One at a time open the cupboards and look inside. Take out one object and hand it to her. Say, "Please put it back." Help her put the object back in its place. Do the same with a dish towel from a drawer, food from the refrigerator, etc. Each time you take out something, ask her to "please put it back." Let her put it back in its place. The idea that everything has a place will make your child feel secure.

Finale

Play this game in a variety of places. In your bedroom you can let your child put socks back in Daddy's drawer, shoes back in a closet, paper back in a desk, etc. In the bathroom she can put a mirror and comb back in a drawer and place towels on a rack.

Encore

Clean out one bottom drawer that can belong to your one-year-old. Let your child help you fill it with a few toys, plastic containers, wooden spoons, and empty food containers. Show your child how to open the drawer. Explain that it is her drawer. You may even want to put her name on an index card or draw a happy face and place it on the outside of the drawer. Explain that the other drawers are not hers and can only be opened and played in when you are there to watch, but this special drawer is a place where she can play whenever she chooses.

Knock It Off!

Thumpaty, thumpaty, thump!
Stumpaty, stumpaty, stump!
—Traditional Rhyme

Overture

Your role as a parent in building activities is to strike a balance between demonstrating new ideas and allowing your toddler to discover on his own. Remember, the goal is to support your toddler's play, not teach a technique of building with blocks.

Performance

Play: To help your toddler learn how to stack a two- or three-block tower, play "Knock It Off!"
What you will need: Wooden blocks
How to play: Place a pile of wooden blocks on the floor between you and your toddler. Stack up three or four blocks and then say, "Knock it off!" Show him how to knock the tower of blocks down. Then stack it up again. Repeat. Soon your toddler will be trying to build towers with two or three blocks. Ask him if you can "knock it off!" Build and knock down small towers together.

Finale

Collecting a variety of construction materials for your toddler can be expensive. Instead, you can use your imagination and collect things in nature and household items. Besides wooden blocks, toddlers like to build with:

◆ Large flat pebbles
◆ Small cardboard boxes with lids taped closed
◆ Smooth pieces of bark
◆ Plastic drinking straws
◆ Empty food containers such as instant gourmet coffee, tea, and cookie tins

Encore

Toddlers do not need a lot of blocks. Creating a set of blocks for your toddler to use can be very satisfying for a parent. Check with a nearby cabinet shop or construction site to see if you can have blocks of scrap lumber. Sand the edges to remove any splinters. Try to obtain some pieces of differently scented woods; cedar and pine have nice aromas. Paint the blocks if you want, or sand and finish them by rubbing with linseed oil. This is a toy you can make for your toddler that may become a family heirloom.

        © Instructional Fair • TS Denison

Sorting Cereals

If all the world were water, and all the water were ink,
What should we do for bread and cheese?
What should we do for drink?
—Traditional Rhyme

Overture

Watch and you will notice that your toddler is acquiring better control with her fingers and hands. Soon she will be able to pick up little things with her index finger and thumb and hold things in her grasp.

Performance

Play: To help your toddler master picking up tiny objects like cereal using the pincher grip, play "Sorting Cereals."
What you will need: Two measuring cups, variety of cereals
How to play: Provide a bowl of a variety of cereals. Include squares, doughnut-shapes, flakes, and special cereals with stars and moon-shaped marshmallow bits in them. Demonstrate how to use the pincher grip to transfer the bits of cereal one at a time from one cup to the other. Your toddler may enjoy many happy moments sorting through the different kinds of cereal. Raisins and other dried fruits may be added to make a trail mix snack.

Finale

When preparing snacks for your toddler, pick foods that will exercise her pincher grip including:
◆ Raisins
◆ Grated cheddar cheese
◆ Bacon bits
◆ Goldfish-shaped crackers
◆ Cooked macaroni
◆ Plain croutons
◆ Chopped prunes
◆ Cooked peas
◆ Banana slices
◆ Ripe pear and peach chunks
◆ Fruit cocktail (Slice the grapes to prevent choking on them.)

Encore

Water and sand play are very good for pincher grip practice. Provide a tub of sand or water and plastic measuring tools: sifter, scoop, spoons, cups, funnels, etc. Pouring, measuring, and sifting are all wonderful activities for practicing eye-hand coordination. With these materials, your toddler will be engaged in hours of educational play.

Fine Motor Development **Twelve- to Eighteen-Month-Old**

Go Fish

One, two, three, four, five,
Catching fishes all alive.
—Traditional Rhyme

Overture

It is estimated that by 11 months, 50% of all toddlers have a pincher grip coordinated enough to pick up raisins. By 12 months, 75% of the toddlers can pick up raisins. And by 15 months, 90% of all toddlers can do it. So if your toddler cannot use his index finger and thumb to pick up tiny things yet, just wait a month or two.

Performance

Play: To help your toddler learn how to take tiny things like raisins out of a tight-fitting container, play "Go Fish."
What you will need: Small container such as a clean film canister, raisins
How to play: Fill the canister with raisins. Demonstrate for your toddler how to use his index finger and thumb to "fish out" the raisins. Each time he pulls out a raisin, tell him to "go fish" for more. Line up the raisins in a row. When they are all out of the container, encourage your child to fill the container again.

Finale

Try "fishing out" other tiny things from small containers including:

◆ Tiny balls of play clay
◆ Cooked, cold pasta
◆ Feathers
◆ Pineapple chunks
◆ Cereal pieces

Encore

Nearly everything your toddler plays with will enhance his fine-motor skills. The smaller the objects of play, the more coordination it will take to handle them. Because of the possibility of swallowing and choking, many small objects are dangerous for toddlers. Other activities to enhance fine-motor coordination include:

◆ Threading big wooden beads on heavy shoelaces
◆ Plastic play people for toddlers
◆ Working with play clay
◆ Painting with finger paints or pudding
◆ Scribbling with a crayon
◆ Turning pages of magazines and books
◆ Looking at old telephone books

Turn the Page, Please

Hush-a-bye, baby, on the treetop,
When the wind blows, the cradle will rock.
—Traditional Rhyme

Overture

Most one-year-olds do not like to sit long enough to hear a story, but they like to look at books and turn pages. Holding your baby and sharing books will be a good way to introduce her to words and teach her to listen and be patient.

Performance

Play: To help teach your toddler how to turn pages of a magazine (three or more at a time) or pages of a board book, play "Turn the Page, Please."

What you will need: Locate a baby board book or a picture book such as *The Puddle* by David M. McPhail (Farrar Straus & Giroux), a book about a boy, animals, and a big puddle.

How to play: Hold your baby in your lap so she can see the pictures and reach to turn the pages of the book. Turn pages and look at the pictures. Then tell your toddler "Turn the page, please." Let her have control over how long you look at each page of the book.

Finale

Board books are specially designed for babies and toddlers. Share a book for a few minutes at bedtime each night, and your toddler will soon cherish this time together.

◆ *Time for Bed* by Mem Fox (Harcourt Brace, 1997)—This delightful 28-page book is about mother animals putting their babies to bed.
◆ *The Going to Bed Book* by Sandra Boynton (Little Simon, 1995)—On board a boat some animals take a bath, put on pajamas, brush their teeth, exercise, and go to bed.
◆ *Hush Little Baby* by Sylvia Long (Chronicle Books, 1997)—A mother rabbit puts her bunnies to bed.

Encore

On other occasions, let your baby practice turning pages of old magazines. Choose magazines with colorful pictures, especially pictures of other children. Toddlers usually turn pages three or more at a time, which is okay. In time and with practice, your toddler will learn how to turn the pages one at a time. To make a special photo collection, fill a photo album with pictures clipped from magazines. Then your toddler can view the pictures without tearing the pages.

Fine Motor Development Twelve- to Eighteen-Month-Old

Play My Face

Nose, nose, jolly red nose;
And what gave thee that jolly red nose?
—Traditional Rhyme

Overture

Watch your one-year-old and you will see he has definite favorites. Given a chance, he can probably pick from several choices. Having a very limited vocabulary and crying a lot less than when he was an infant, pointing is the way he can tell you what he wants.

Performance

Play: To give your toddler practice using his index finger to point, play "Play My Face."
What you will need: No special equipment is needed to play this game.
How to play: Put your baby on your lap facing you so he can see your face. Make up a different sound for each part of your face.
Examples:

- ◆ Touch nose. (Sneeze.)
- ◆ Touch lips. (Honk.)
- ◆ Touch eyebrows. (Buzz.)
- ◆ Touch chin. (Click tongue.)
- ◆ Touch an ear lob. (Squeak.)
- ◆ Touch cheeks. (Whistle loudly.)

Touch places on your face with an index finger and make the appropriate sounds. Then let your toddler use an index finger to touch your face. Each time he touches you, make a silly sound. Make silly sounds as you touch parts of his face, too.

Finale

Play the same game by having the baby touch different body parts and then make movements instead of sounds.
Examples:

- ◆ Touch knee. (Lift lower part of leg as if reflexed.)
- ◆ Touch hand. (Clap.)
- ◆ Touch arm. (Flap arms like flying.)
- ◆ Touch stomach. (Giggle.)

Encore

Rituals are especially enjoyable for one-year-olds. Begin your own silly sound ritual. Invent a sound that the two of you make that means something to both of you—a sound that no one else will understand. It might be something you say to soothe him when he is afraid, or a secret way you have to say "I love you." It does not matter what the sound is or what it means, the important thing is that you and your toddler have this secret connection.

© Instructional Fair • TS Denison

Paper Wads

Tit, tat, toe,
My first go.
—Traditional Rhyme

Overture

Watch your toddler playing, and you will see she is learning about space, shape, and size. She is interested in how things relate to each other. Affecting the shape of objects such as wadding up a sheet of paper will become fascinating to your toddler as she gets closer to her year and-a-half birthday.

Performance

Play: To help your toddler learn how to coordinate hands and fingers, wad paper into balls.
What you will need: Sheets of newspaper, large grocery bag (fold down the edges to make a sturdy container)
How to play: Show your toddler how to wad a sheet of paper into a ball. Toss it into the grocery bag. If wadding is too difficult, begin the wads and shape them into balls for her. Let her squeeze them to make them smaller. Then help her put the wadded paper into the grocery bag. When she is finished wadding up as many sheets as she wants, help her carry the bag of papers to the recycling bin and dump it.

Finale

Paper holds a great deal of fascination for toddlers. Try some of these paper activities that will encourage the use of fine motor skills.
- Fold paper airplanes, then let your toddler fly them. Show her how to launch them.
- Cut simple snowflakes and let her unfold them.
- Cut strings of paper dolls and let her unfold them.
- Show her how to rip strips of paper.
- Use a hole punch to make paper dots. Have her try to pick them up and put them in a cup.
- Give her old mail with envelopes so she can pretend she has mail.
- Give her old magazines to examine.
- Show her how to fold paper.

Encore

Provide interesting paper for your toddler's play including:
- Crepe paper streamers (taped to a paper straw)
- Cellophane (taped inside a cardboard frame like a color lens)
- Tissue paper to fold and wad
- Aluminum foil
- Textured wallpaper samples (cut into 6"–8" [15–20 cm] squares)
- Old gift wrap (crumpled and unfolded flat again)
- Large sheets cut from sides of grocery bags

Fine Motor Development **Twelve- to Eighteen-Month-Old**

Toss

Bring the hoop, and bring the ball,
Come with happy faces all.
—Traditional Rhyme

Overture

Watch your toddler playing with balls, and you will see that each day his eye-hand coordination is improving. His ability to use his hands to "catch" and throw objects will progress as he gets more and more practice.

Performance

Play: To help your toddler practice letting go of something at will, play "Toss."
What you will need: Whiffle ball or soft ball
How to play: Stand about a yard (meter) from a wall or fence. Toss a whiffle ball toward the wall. Retrieve the ball and give it to your toddler. Tell him to toss the ball. Each time he tosses the ball toward the wall, retrieve it for him.

Finale

To practice letting go, toss other objects, such as:

- ◆ Beanbag
- ◆ Beach ball
- ◆ Badminton birdie
- ◆ Large paper airplane
- ◆ Tennis ball
- ◆ Flying disc

Encore

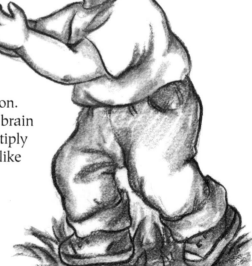

Toddlers are just learning how to get their bodies to do what they want them to do. To release the grip on something does not happen automatically for a toddler. For example, when a one-year-old wants to let go of a ball, his fingers may not release without great concentration. His expansion of playing and thinking reflects underlying brain growth. Connections between the nerves in the brain multiply rapidly between birth and age two. Performing actions like tossing or catching a ball builds certain connections.

Catch

Let us make a merry ring,
Talk and laugh, and dance and sing.
—Traditional Rhyme

Overture

In the beginning, walking is a matter of using hands and arms as well as feet and legs. Staying balanced is so difficult, your toddler will use her arms and hands for balance and support.

Performance

Play: To offer your toddler an opportunity to practice coordinating both hands to catch a large object such as a beach ball, play "Catch."

What you will need: Beach ball

How to play: Sit on the floor approximately a yard (meter) from your toddler. Gently roll the beach ball to her. Demonstrate how to catch the ball using both hands. As you roll the ball toward your toddler, tell her "catch." Signal her when it is time to extend her arms and get ready to catch the ball. Practice rolling the ball back and forth.

Finale

Show your toddler how to stop a ball by putting up her hands. Play a gentle game of batting the beach ball with hands. Toss the ball and have your toddler, instead of trying to catch the ball, hit the ball with open hands. Retrieve the ball and gently toss it to her again. This adaptation of volley ball may seem boring to you, but it will be very exciting for your toddler to see that she can "with the wave of a hand" change the direction of the ball. It will help her practice lifting her arms and opening and closing her hands.

Encore

Activities that encourage the toddler to use her hands in a coordinated way will strengthen her eye-hand coordination. Doing some form of hand exercises where the child connects the verbal instruction with an exercise she sees demonstrated will be enjoyable and educational. Try some of these hand exercises:

- ◆ Holding up both hands at once—Open, close, open, close, etc.
- ◆ Holding up one finger at a time—Up, down, up, down, etc.
- ◆ Holding up thumbs—Up, down, up, down, etc.
- ◆ Holding up both hands at once—Spread fingers apart, close, apart, close, etc.
- ◆ Holding up both hands at once—Bend at wrist, straighten, bend, straighten, etc.
- ◆ Holding the base of the palms together to clap—Open fingers, close fingers, etc.
- ◆ Intertwining fingers—Squeeze, relax, squeeze, relax, squeeze, etc.

Fine Motor Development **Twelve- to Eighteen-Month-Old**

Treasure Box

Now you see it,
Now you don't.

Overture

Watch your toddler and you may see that everything seems magical to him. He believes in magic and is always ready for the unexpected. He does not know what will happen next, so all things seem like a big surprise.

Performance

Play: To give your toddler the opportunity to open a small hinged box, play "Treasure Box."

What you will need: Plastic pencil box, a new small toy that will fit inside the box

How to play: Sit with the toddler. Show him the box that has the toy hidden inside. Ask him what he thinks might be inside the box. Build up the suspense. Then let him lift the lid to find out what is hidden inside the box. Allow your child to play with it.

Finale

Use three hinged boxes to play this guessing game. Place the boxes in front of your toddler. Let him watch you put something inside one of the boxes. Then ask him which box has the object inside it. Although he watched you put the object in a box, it may be difficult for him to remember which box holds the object. He has no language yet to tell himself, "The ball is in the middle box" or "The ball is in the first box." Play this game several times. Let him open the boxes each time to search for the object. Then let him hide an object and you guess where it is hidden.

Encore

When playing games with hidden objects inside a box, teach your toddler to use clues to finding the object. For example, show him how to lift the box and shake it and listen to hear if something is inside it. Have him close his eyes. Put a ball inside a box. Then have him hold each box and see if he can tell which one contains the ball.

Keeping Track

Milestone	Date	Comments
Can handle objects with care and gentleness		
Can turn light switches on and off		
Can fill and empty containers		
Can hold something in both hands at once		
Can grasp two things in hands at once		
Can put things back where they belong		
Can stack a two- or three-block tower		
Can pick up tiny things with pincher grasp		
Can take tiny things out of a small container		
Can turn pages of a magazine and book		
Can use index finger to point		
Can make a paper wad		
Can let go of objects at will		
Can use both hands together to hold something		
Can open a small box with hinged lid		

All By Myself

Gross Motor Development

Contemplate

During the second year of life, your baby will go through a remarkable transformation—she will become a toddler. The dramatic leap in development that will occur between her one-year and one-and-a-half-year birthdays will involve a myriad of physical, emotional, and cognitive advances, but her physical advances will be those most evident to you.

As your toddler begins to sit, stand, and walk alone, she will rapidly develop new motor skills. She may be rather cautious, but with the support of the parent she will play with new vigor. She will be most interested in lifting and swinging games, jumping, wrestling, and all sorts of physical exchanges between herself and others. She will often initiate the games and always want to test her new strengths. The best place for parents and toddlers to play vigorously will be outside—better yet at a playground or park. To allow your toddler an opportunity to practice gross motor skills each day, make sure she has plenty of physical exercise.

Gross Motor Milestones: Twelve to Eighteen Months

- ◆ Will begin to move in rhythm
- ◆ Will begin to pretend play
- ◆ Will learn how to crawl over a low barrier
- ◆ Will learn to climb up the stairs on hands and knees
- ◆ Will learn to slide down the stairs backwards on tummy
- ◆ Will learn to sit down from a free-standing position
- ◆ Will be able to sit alone and pivot at the waist to look in all directions
- ◆ Will learn to sit in a child-sized chair for a short period
- ◆ Will learn to stand up without support
- ◆ Will enjoy playing rough and tumble games
- ◆ Will learn to stoop and pick up objects while holding onto something with one hand
- ◆ Will learn to walk
- ◆ Will learn to climb out of high chair, crib, stroller, etc.
- ◆ Will learn how to throw a small ball
- ◆ Will learn how to jump with an adult holding her hands for support

 General Tips

Physical games are more important than for just practicing gross motor skills. They are an opportunity for intimacy—wrestling, hugging, touching. What will make the play special for your toddler is that he is sharing it with you. His favorite games will be those with personal touches. Spontaneity is the key ingredient when playing with your toddler. Games that grow out of the spirit of the moment will be the most fun for you and your child.

The games in this book are just a beginning for ways to exercise and practice new skills. As you and your toddler play the games, adapt them to your own personal liking. You might alter them by:

- ◆ Including a personalized song or favorite rhyme
- ◆ Adding silly, nonsense sounds
- ◆ Wearing some matching hats, bandanas, or caps that mean "we are a team"
- ◆ Playing the same game with unique, inventive props (instead of using a ball, use a banana, and so on)
- ◆ Laughing a lot while playing
- ◆ Talking to your toddler about the game after you finish playing and describing to others how the two of you played the game
- ◆ Taking photographs of your toddler playing the games and later talking about the photographs with your toddler
- ◆ Including other children in the games
- ◆ Having a sibling or other parent watch as you and your toddler play a particular game

Appropriate toys for developing a one-year-old's gross motor skills include:

- ◆ Beginner's tricycle
- ◆ Outdoor toys like small slides and swings
- ◆ Sandbox
- ◆ Sand measuring tools such as plastic cups, spoons, bowls, scoops
- ◆ Digging toys for sand play such as bucket, shovel, rake
- ◆ Pull and push toys
- ◆ Large cardboard boxes
- ◆ Balls of all shapes and sizes

Boing

Spring up, spring down,
Boing, boing, all around.

Overture

Watch your one-year-old's motor skills from day to day, and you will see big leaps in his abilities. What you will not be able to see at first glance is how his imagination is developing. During this developmental stage, your toddler will begin using his imagination when playing games—pretending and making believe.

Performance

Play: Offer your toddler an opportunity to move in rhythm. Play "Boing."

What you will need: Music with a fast, clear beat

How to play: Explain to your toddler how you will be moving up and down like a spring. (Show him a spring if you have one available.) Turn on the music. Hold your toddler's hands to support his standing position. Keep feet stationary and move from the knees up. Then bob up and down from the waist. Each time you spring up and down, make the sound a spring makes—"boing." Try springing your shoulders up and down. Keep time to the music. Just for fun, hold your toddler in your arms and spring up and down by bouncing off the floor with your feet together. Move to the music like Winnie the Pooh's friend Tigger.

Finale

Toddlers love rhythm toys and playing with sounds, music, rhythmic instruments. A tambourine, musical triangle with striker, rhythm sticks, and a small drum can be purchased in educational toy stores or some music stores. Look for special children's recordings and classical music, too. Show your toddler how to play a rhythm instrument. Encourage rhythmic play.

Encore

Although your toddler will present you with many new challenges, he will also be an entertaining addition to the family. He will begin to have a self-awareness that will lead to a sense of humor. Your toddler already knows he can become the center of attention by being "cute." He will especially like dancing and moving to music because it puts him smack dab in the middle of the spotlight. Allow him many opportunities to "show off" for family and friends. He will soon develop his own dance of springing up and down, tipping his head from side to side, and swinging his arms. Along with the challenges presented by a child this age, you will be compensated with the company of a fun-loving, humorous partner who is always ready to play.

© Instructional Fair • TS Denison

Peekaboo Box

Knock, knock, where are you?
Peekaboo, I see you!

Overture

Sometime during the first half of your baby's second year, she will begin to demonstrate a glimmering of imagination. She may pretend to drink from an empty cup or pretend to eat a wooden block. You can encourage make-believe play and pretending, too.

Performance

Play: To encourage your toddler to pretend, play "Peekaboo Box."
What you will need: Large cardboard box (bigger than your toddler)
How to play: Put the box on its side so the top flaps can be opened and closed on one side like a door. Help your baby get inside the box. Then close the flaps. Open and say "Peekaboo." Each time you open the box and find your toddler, act surprised. "What are you doing in there?" "Where did you go?"

Finale

Pretending with your toddler will let her know that fantasy play is fun and can be shared. When playing with your toddler pantomime these familiar events:

- ◆ Eating and drinking
- ◆ Sleeping
- ◆ Leaving and arriving home
- ◆ Dressing and undressing
- ◆ Driving a car
- ◆ Riding on a school bus, air-plane, or boat

Encore

Build and play in special hiding places with your toddler including:

- ◆ Blanket tent
- ◆ Cardboard playhouse
- ◆ Clothesline and sheet tepee
- ◆ Pillow cave
- ◆ Behind the sofa hideaway
- ◆ Under the cupboard compartments
- ◆ Under the bed bunker

Superman

Faster than a speeding bullet,
More powerful than a locomotive,
Able to leap tall buildings at a single bound . . .
—Jerry Siegel and Joe Shuster

Overture

Watch your toddler as he crawls. As soon at he masters the skills it takes to coordinate arms, legs, and balancing his body, he will gain agility and speed. He will suddenly become faster, more powerful, and able to leap low barriers in a single bound.

Performance

Play: To give your toddler practice crawling over a low barrier, play "Superman."

What you will need: Short cape that will not get hung up under his legs, pillows, small cardboard boxes, stuffed animals

How to play: Build an obstacle course with pillows, boxes, and stuffed animals. Safety pin the Superman cape on your toddler (be sure the cape does not hamper your child's movements); perhaps wear one yourself. Crawl around the course. Have your toddler follow you until he knows how to weave in, out, and over the obstacles.

Finale

Play "Crawling Tag" with your toddler (not wearing short cape). As in regular tag, one person chases after the other and when tagged, the tagged person becomes the chaser. The only difference in "Crawling Tag" is you are both on your hands and knees. Chances are, your toddler will be faster at crawling than you are. Use the obstacle course to play a chase game round and round. Also have some crawling races in the grass. It is good that your toddler will see that he can move faster than you on hands and knees.

Encore

While you are down on the floor, play some wrestling, rough-and-tumble games with your toddler.

- Give him a ride on your back.
- Flat on your back, raise him up with your feet on his tummy.
- Be a bridge and let him crawl under, around, and climb over you.
- Get him in a bear hug and see if he can get loose.

© Instructional Fair • TS Denison

London Bridge

London Bridge is falling down,
Falling down, falling down.
London Bridge is falling down,
My fair lady!
—Traditional Rhyme

Overture

Watch your toddler as she looks around while standing up. Your toddler's field of vision from a new vantage point will bring her new perspectives, great pleasures, and a little anxiety about how to get back down. Your toddler's desire for this stand-up view will motivate her to spend more and more time up where she can see things better.

Performance

Play: To help your toddler practice standing up and balancing herself, play this variation of "London Bridge."

What you will need: An area for play where the floor is padded with carpet, a thick quilt, or the best option, in the grass

How to play: Stand your toddler up and hold both her hands. Slowly move in a circle, singing the song. Follow the directions:

London Bridge is falling down, (*Holding hands, circle around.*)
Falling down, falling down. (*Continue holding hands and circling.*)
London Bridge is falling down, (*Drop hands and sit down.*)
My fair lady! (*Lie back on the floor to rest.*)

Stand up and hold the toddler's hands and begin again.

Finale

After your toddler can stand alone without holding your hands, play a version of the game without holding her hands. Bob up and down on the first two lines and swing arms freely. Sit down on the third line; lie back on the floor to rest on the last line.

Encore

When your toddler can walk and is steady on her feet, play this game another way.

London Bridge is falling down, (*Two people stand and hold hands and make a bridge with arms.*)
Falling down, falling down. (*Toddler circles around and under the "bridge."*)
London Bridge is falling down, (*Toddler keeps circling around and under.*)
My fair lady! (*Bring down arms and trap the toddler inside the "bridge."*)

Now sing the second verse: Take the key and lock her up, lock her up, lock her up. Take the key and lock her up, my fair lady!

Up, Up, and Away!

Upward and onward,
Like a goose with a stiff upper lip.

Overture

Watch your toddler exploring new territory like stairs. His expanded locomotor capacity will broaden his world. Nothing will stop him now. Even stairs may not seem like a challenge. Working with your toddler to teach him how to get up and down the stairs will help him avoid falling. When learning to ascend stairs, always spot your child for safety.

Performance

Play: To give your toddler practice climbing carpeted stairs on hands and knees, play "Up, Up, and Away!"

What you will need: Place to practice on carpeted stairs, favorite toy

How to play: Your toddler will have to be a proficient crawler before he can learn to climb stairs on his hands and knees. Begin by placing him on his hands and knees at the bottom of the stairs. Place a favorite toy two or three steps above his reach. Encourage him to go up. Say, "Up, up, and away." Bend over and hold him at the waist and tell him again, "Up, up, and away!" Then steer him upward. If need be, hold onto him so he will feel secure. Keep urging him to continue until he reaches the top of the stairs. Say something like, "Upward and onward, like a goose with a stiff upper lip." When he gets to the top, he will want to see the giant "mountain" he has scaled. Praise your mountain climber. Tell him how big he is and how strong he is growing. Applaud his accomplishment. Repeat several times each day for a week or more before you allow him to try it on his own. The first few times he does it without your hands on his waist, stand on the steps next to him. Practice unassisted climbing for a while before allowing him to do it without you nearby.

Finale

Toddlers have no sense of distance or danger; they will try to climb up onto everything that appears promising. Tables, bookcases, cupboards, beds, and sofas will all look like new adventures for them. You can help your toddler learn how to get down from high places by teaching him the sliding-down-on-your-stomach method. Use a low sofa and the cushions to create steps to scale. Place two cushions on top of each other next to the sofa. Place one cushion in front of them creating a soft stair-effect. Let your toddler play on the three levels and practice moving forward and upward at the same time.

Encore

Undoubtedly, your toddler's favorite thing to scale will be you. Rough-and tumble games will be among his favorites. Getting on your hands and knees on the floor and letting him set the pace for the game will be fun, and it will provide him with the gross motor exercise that he needs. Encourage him to try to climb up onto your back. Once on your back, have him wrap his hands around your neck and have a bucking bronco ride. Be gentle at first and as he learns the game and can grasp more tightly, move a little more vigorously.

114

Going Down

Going down,
down, down,
d
      o
          w
              n.

Overture

Never underestimate the motivation your child gets from attention and praise. All new skills will be strengthened by your adulation. Applaud your toddler often and watch her face. Nothing will make her so happy or proud as pleasing you.

Performance

Play: To help your toddler learn how to slide down stairs backwards on her tummy, play "Going Down."

What you will need: Place to practice on carpeted stairs

How to play: Your toddler will have to be proficient at crawling up the stairs before she can learn to slide down the stairs on her tummy. If she is a good crawler, you can play a game to teach her how to get down stairs safely. Place her on her hands and knees on the top stair. Bend over and hold her at the waist and tell her "going down." Guide her into a slide down the stairs. Use your hands to slow down her momentum because moving too quickly backwards down the stairs will be scary for her. When she reaches the bottom stair, tell her "Up, up, and away" and let her crawl up the stairs on her own. Repeat many times until she can safely slide down the stairs on her belly.

Finale

You can teach your toddler to get down off sofas and beds the same way she gets down the stairs—on her belly. Place her on her stomach with feet hanging off the sofa or bed. Lower her slowly with your hands around her waist until her feet touch the floor. Then show her how to hold onto the sofa or bed and lower herself into a sitting position. Repeat several times a day until she gets proficient at getting down off sofas and beds.

Encore

Providing a wide range of physical challenges will help your toddler feel good about herself. Although she is not old enough to use playground equipment independently, she can enjoy them in your arms or with you holding her hands. She can experience sliding down a slide with you behind her holding onto her as you go down. When swinging, try holding her in your lap, facing you. Place one arm around her and use the other arm to hold the swing. The merry-go-round also can be enjoyed as long as you are right there by her side.

Ring-Around the Rosy

Ring-around the rosy,
Pocket full of posies.
Ashes, ashes, all fall down.
—Traditional Rhyme

Overture

Watch your toddler when he is first learning to stand, and you may see the excitement on his face turn to fear when it is time to sit back down. Usually a toddler will just drop with a loud plop on his bottom. No matter how thick the diaper, it still has to hurt! There are things you can teach your toddler that will soften the blow.

Performance

Play: To teach your toddler how to sit down painlessly from a free-standing position, play "Ring-Around the Rosy."
What you will need: Pillow
How to play: Place a large, soft pillow on the floor where you will be playing. Holding your toddler's hands, help him stand up. Still holding onto his hands, demonstrate how to bend at the knees and sit in a squat. Then placing hands on the floor for support, land in a soft-plop. Repeat this exercise several times each day for awhile, until you see your toddler using the soft-plop on his own.

Finale

To practice the soft-plop, use the rhyme "Ring-Around the Rosy" to play a game. Hold your toddler's hands and move in a circle as you sing the song.
Follow the directions:

Ring-around the rosy, (*Turn round and round.*)
Pocket full of posies. (*Keeping turning around.*)
Ashes, ashes, (*Bend at the knees and sit in a squ...*
All fall down. (*Gently plop down.*)

Encore

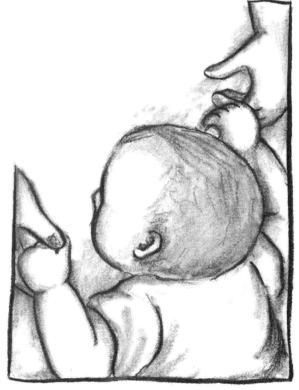

On other occasions, teach your toddler other ways leave a standing position including:

◆ Bend knees and sit in a squat. Place hands in front and lower onto knees. Crawl off.
◆ Bend knees and sit in a squat. Lean one shoulder to the floor.
◆ Bend knees and sit in a squat. Place hands in front and lower onto knees. Straighten legs out underneath and lie flat on stomach.
◆ Bend knees and sit in a squat. Use hands to help fall into a gentle plop. Stretch legs out front and lower back to the floor. Rest flat on back.

© Instructional Fair • TS Denison

Gotcha!

Don't look now, Here I come.
Don't look at me. . . . Gotcha!

Overture

Watch and you will notice that your toddler is always watching what is happening around her. Sitting up will give her more visibility because she can turn her head and pivot her body to see in all directions.

Performance

Play: To help your toddler get practice sitting without assistance and pivoting while sitting, play "Gotcha!"

What you will need: Stuffed teddy bear

How to play: Place your toddler sitting up on a soft surface like a padded quilt or the grass. On hands and knees, go behind her. "Walk" the teddy bear on the blanket to the left of your toddler. Then tap her on the nose with it while saying, "Gotcha!" When toddler gets calm, perform the same action on her right side. Sneak up on one or the other side with "gotcha" until she tires of the game. She will have to pivot to see the bear as it "walks" up to her. If you get very still and just pause, your toddler will pivot almost completely around so she can see what you are doing and from where you are coming. This is good exercise for her lower back, shoulder, and neck muscles.

Finale

Play the same "Gotcha!" game and add the possibility of coming up over your toddler's head. This third possibility will add excitement to the game and also be good exercise for your toddler's neck muscles. It is more difficult to stay balanced when lifting eyes and head upward. Be prepared for the possibility that your toddler will fall backwards when lifting her head upward.

Encore

"Gotcha!" can be played in a variety of places. Try some of these variations:

◆ Place your toddler on a large bed. Crawl on the floor around the bed. Pop up and say, "Gotcha!"
◆ Place your toddler in a large, overstuffed chair. Get behind the chair and pop up on the sides or from overhead and say, "Gotcha!"
◆ While the toddler is in her crib, use the teddy bear to jump up somewhere—"Gotcha!"

Gross Motor Development Twelve- to Eighteen-Month-Old

Rock-a-Bye, Baby

Rock-a-bye, baby, in the treetop.
When the wind blows the cradle will rock.
—Traditional Rhyme

Overture

Play is a toddler's most powerful way of learning. Having her own child-sized furniture will give her props for learning to sit up, rock back and forth, and balance herself.

Performance

Play: To reinforce sitting on a small chair for short periods, play "Rock-a-Bye, Baby."
What you will need: Child-sized chair or rocking chair; small, soft rag doll
How to play: Place your toddler in the chair or rocking chair. Give him the doll to hold like a baby. Show him how to rock back and forth and sing to the "baby." Balancing in the chair and rocking back and forth while holding something in his arms will take a great deal of coordination. Your toddler may need his arms free to balance. Place your toddler in the chair several times a day for practice while you are nearby for support.

Finale

Getting into and out of a small chair also takes gross motor skills. Since your toddler is just learning to stand up and stay balanced while upright, pushing off from a small chair will need to be practiced. At first he may just slide out of the chair onto the floor. Help him make soft landings. It is important that your toddler has child-sized furniture. The more scaled down you can make his furniture, the easier it will be for him to learn how to be at comfortable places, other than the floor, and the more independent he will feel.

Encore

One-year-olds should have dolls. Even boy babies should have dolls for play. Some of the soft, simple dolls appropriate for infants can also be used for young toddlers. Your toddler may want a more realistic baby doll for his first pretend play. Vinyl or rubber baby dolls are appropriate for this age. The doll should be of simple construction without hair or moveable eyes. Clothes should also be simple and need not be detachable because toddlers cannot dress and undress a doll yet. Dolls should be small enough to hold and carry around in one hand.

© Instructional Fair • TS Denison

Drop the Hankie

Little Lord Frankie,
Has lost his hankie.

Overture

Watch your toddler playing repetitious games, and you will see that she likes knowing what will happen next. Games that you might think are very boring will hold great delight for your one-year-old.

Performance

Play: To help your toddler learn how to stoop and pick up an object from the floor while holding on with one hand, play "Drop the Hankie."

What you will need: Cotton hankie or silk scarf

How to play: Hold your toddler's hand and walk along. Pretend to accidentally drop the hankie and ask, "Where did I drop the hankie?" While holding one of the toddler's hands, find the hankie and let her stoop over and pick it up. Tell her thank you. Then walk along some more. Drop the hankie again. Repeat steps, each time letting the toddler retrieve the hankie. Always act surprised that you cannot find it and pleased when she gives it back to you.

Finale

When you take your toddler for a walk, she will often want to stop and scoop up something she sees. Encourage her curiosity and desire to collect natural things found on the ground such as:

◆ Pretty pebbles (large enough that she cannot put them into her mouth)
◆ Colorful leaves of all shapes and sizes
◆ Bird feathers
◆ Seashells on the beach

Encore

Distinguishing between what your toddler can take and what does not belong to her will be taught in many stages at different occasions. Telling her when it is okay to pick up something and take it home will help her make the distinction.

◆ Teach your toddler that picking up some things from the ground is okay but picking things off trees, bushes, or plants is not okay.
◆ When shopping in the supermarket, take along a bag of snacks for your toddler so she will not want to eat what you are putting into the shopping cart. Allowing your toddler to sample fruits, etc., in the market sends a wrong message about what is and what is not hers.
◆ When browsing stores with interesting items, teach your toddler how to look without touching. When it is okay to touch, for example in a toy store, make the distinction for her by telling her it is okay to touch while you are there to help her.
◆ Teach her that in some places it is okay to touch, such as in a library. Teach your toddler that looking at books is okay. Help her know which books are for children and where she can sit and look at the books she chooses.

Walk the Baby

Standing with reluctant feet,
Where the brook and river meet,
Womanhood and childhood fleet!
—Henry Wadsworth Longfellow

Overture

In the developmental stage of one- to one-and-a-half-years old, your toddler will move from an awkward, upright standing position to walking with support to being able to walk without support.

Performance

Play: To give your toddler gross motor practice, walk with your child every day.
What you will need: No special equipment is needed for this activity.
How to play: Weather permitting, take your toddler for a walk outside every day. Hold his hand for support if he wants it. If not, stay close to catch him if he runs into problems. Exciting places to visit include:

- Park
- Police station
- Auto repair garage
- Airport
- Fire station
- Newspaper office
- Bakery
- Zoo

Finale

Remember, your toddler's learning can rise no higher than his experiences. The broader his experiences, the better his education will be. So take him to places where he can see exciting things. When weather does not permit walking outside, try some of these interesting places to take walks:

- In the mall
- In the library
- Around in a store
- In a gym or grade school cafeteria
- In a nursing home to visit residents
- In a hospital to have lunch
- In a museum
- In a conservatory

Encore

Do not be surprised if your toddler decides to try walking backward. Although walking forward is still a challenge, he may find walking so exciting that he will try other kinds of locomotion. Running will not be smooth, but when in a hurry his walking may turn into running. His good feelings about mastering the difficult skill of walking will empower him in many other ways.

  © Instructional Fair • TS Denison

Flying Baby

Toss up my darling, toss him up high,
Don't let his head, though, hit the blue sky.
—Traditional Rhyme

Overture

Some games that people play with babies are as old as the hills. One that nearly everyone has played with babies is tossing them up in the air. Toddlers enjoy being lifted high into the air and swung around. Rough and tumble games provide a perfect opportunity for your child to experience "up," "down," "around," and "under."

Performance

Play: To pleasure your toddler with a rough and tumble game, play "Flying Baby."

What you will need: No special equipment is needed to play this game.

How to play: Use both hands to hold your toddler under the arms. Lift her high into the air. Hold her up where she can see things from this new vantage point. Slowly turn in a 360 degree circle so she can see everything. Gently lower her. Ask her if she wants to fly up again. Some babies like to ride around high up in the air. Play "Flying Baby" by walking from room to room with your baby high overhead. When you come to a door, you may need to dip her down a bit to get under the doorway. When you lower her, say, "Down." When you raise her, say, "Up." When you turn her around, say, "Round and round."

Finale

Another rough and tumble game one-year-olds enjoy is swinging around. Hold your toddler under the arms and spin in a circle so her feet and legs swing out parallel with the ground. Do not hold the toddler by her hands and spin around; it pulls too much on shoulder and wrist ligaments. After spinning the toddler around, place her on her feet and hold her hands for awhile until she is no longer dizzy, or help her down into a sitting position so she can rest.

Encore

Some toddlers enjoy seeing the world spin around them and will spin themselves in circles until they are too dizzy to stand up. Others like to ride around on the shoulders or back of a parent. You and your toddler will devise games that delight and excite her. Try a variety of wrestling, lifting, and carrying games. Your toddler will let you know which ones she likes and which ones are too scary for her.

Gross Motor Development **Twelve- to Eighteen-Month-Old**

Hold On Tight

Hold on, hold on tight,
This is a hold on, hold-up!

Overture

Watch your toddler during the next few months. Soon she will be trying to climb out of the high chair, crib, and stroller. When the toddler wants to get down, she may no longer cry or call for your help. Instead, she may try to maneuver herself to where she wants to be. This can be dangerous.

Performance

Play: To help your toddler learn how to climb safely out of the high chair, crib, and stroller, teach her how to trust her own grip. Play "Hold On Tight."

What you will need: No special equipment is needed to play this game.

How to play: Stand facing your toddler. Place each of your index fingers in the palms of her hands. Tell her to "hold tight." Slowly lift her half an inch (13 mm) off the floor. Remind her to "hold tight." Hold her there for two to five seconds. Slowly lower her back to the floor. Ask her if she likes the game. If she wants to play again, lift her an inch (25 mm) off the floor and hold her there for five seconds. Repeat holding her up a few inches (several centimeters) from the floor and extending the time she has to hold on to six or seven seconds. Playing this game will teach her to trust her own grip.

Finale

Toddlers like to challenge their own strength—test their limits. Take your toddler to a playground and hold her so she can grip bars and move from rung to rung. Do not let go, just let her exercise hands, fingers, and arms on the bars as you carry her.

Encore

As your toddler progresses from one to two years of age, she will begin to be more impatient. In her hurriedness to get from place to place, she will sometimes take a few spills. Taking time to teach your toddler how to back out of the crib, high chair, and stroller by holding on tightly until her feet touch the ground will save her some inevitable falls. Holding onto her waist, take her through the steps. Remind her to "hold tight." Practicing these kinds of gross motor exercises will seem like a game. Make it fun by praising her successes.

Toss It

One for the money, two for the show.
Three to make ready, four to go.
—Traditional Rhyme

Overture..

Watch your toddler playing with a small ball. Learning to release the ball was a difficult skill to acquire. Coordinating the letting go of the ball with bending the elbow and extending the arm all at the same time takes practice. Playing ball with your toddler is the best way he can learn this skill.

Performance..

Play: To practice throwing a small ball by bending the elbow and extending the arm, play "Toss It."
What you will need: Tennis ball
How to play: Show your toddler how to toss a tennis ball. Tennis balls are good balls to use with toddlers because they are soft and small enough that toddlers can get a pretty good grip on them. Have your toddler toss the ball to you. Hand it back to him so he can toss it to you again. Do not expect your toddler to be able to catch a small ball. To avoid frustrating him, hand him the ball instead of throwing it to him. To turn the tossing into a game, use the rhyme. On the word "go" he is to toss the ball.

One for the money, (*Hand him the ball.*)
Two for the show. (*Wait.*)
Three to make ready, (*Wait.*)
Four to go. (*Bend elbow, extend arm, and release the ball.*)

Finale ....

To give your toddler practice bending his knee and kicking a ball, play this simple version of soccer. Play in front of a wall so he will not have to walk far to retrieve the ball. Place the large rubber ball in front of your toddler. Then stand behind the child, and hold his hands up over his head. Show him how to bend one of his knees and kick the ball. Continue holding his hands so he will not fall over when he lifts up one leg to kick the ball. After he has kicked the ball and regained his balance, let him run after the ball. Place the ball on the ground again and repeat the process.

Encore ....

Remember, your toddler is still getting used to the upright position. It will take some time before he can lift up one leg to kick, hop, or skip without losing his balance. Holding his hands as he practices these new ways of moving will help him learn more quickly.

Jump!

Jack be nimble, Jack be quick,
And Jack jump over the candlestick.
—Traditional Rhyme

Overture

Toddlers like to jump off things. Heights will not frighten her. When you least expect it, your child might decide to jump into your arms. Teaching your toddler to warn you with the word "Jump!" will give you time to react. Teach your child how to say "jump" with this activity.

Performance

Play: To give your toddler practice jumping off the floor with both feet together, play "Jump!"
What you will need: No special equipment is needed to play this game.
How to play: Stand behind your toddler. Holding her hands above her head, tell her to "Jump!" Then pick her up slightly so she is off the ground for a split second. Each time you are going to jump her off the ground, tell her "Jump!" Your toddler will love jumping around the house with you as her parachute.

Finale

Toddlers, like all children, love to jump on beds. Mini-trampolines are also favorites. Encourage your toddler's jumping by giving her an opportunity to jump on a bed or trampoline. Share the rhyme "Ten Little Monkeys" with her. Hold her hands as she jumps to the beat of the rhyme.

Ten little monkeys jumping on the bed,
One fell off and broke his head.
Momma called the doctor and the doctor said,
"No more monkeys jumping on the bed."
Nine little monkeys jumping on the bed,
One fell off and broke his head.
Momma called the doctor and the doctor said,
"No more monkeys jumping on the bed."
Eight little monkeys jumping on the bed,
One fell off and broke his head.
Momma called the doctor and the doctor said,
"No more monkeys jumping on the bed." (Continue until no monkeys are left.)

The rhyme can be done also as a finger play. Hold ten fingers up and move your hands up and down like they are jumping on the bed. Then put one finger down to make nine monkeys. Use your hands as if you are talking on the telephone to show when Momma calls the doctor.

Encore

Go puddle jumping. The next time it rains be sure to take your toddler out, hold her hands above her head and her "jump" over the puddles.

© Instructional Fair • TS Denison

Keeping Track

Milestone	Date	Comments
Can move in rhythm		
Can engage in pretend play		
Can crawl over low barriers		
Can climb up stairs on hands and knees		
Can slide down stairs on stomach		
Can sit down from free-standing position		
Can sit alone and pivot around		
Can sit up in a child-sized chair		
Can stand up and balance while upright		
Can participate in rough-and-tumble play		
Can stoop and pick up objects while supported		
Can walk		
Can climb out of the crib, high chair, or stroller		
Can throw a ball		
With support, can jump off the floor		

"Dada, Mama"

Language Development

Contemplate

Although your toddler cannot speak yet, he can understand most of what he hears. His language development at this stage is not speaking words but matching objects and words—comprehension.

With your toddler's new understanding of words will come an opportunity to really communicate with him. You can tell him stories, share your thoughts, and get him to do things. A high-pitched, singsong voice will no longer be appropriate. You may still share "baby talk" with him when he is sleepy or sick, but basically, your conversations with your one-year-old will be on a new level.

Remember, you are your child's language model. The more you talk to him, the more you share with him, the more he will have to comprehend and the quicker he will master language. When speaking to your toddler, keep these simple rules in mind:
- Use the correct terms for things.
- Speak slowly and clearly.
- Use simple words and short sentences.
- Make things concrete by pointing to objects and naming them.

Language Milestones: Twelve to Eighteen Months

- Will begin to enjoy listening to short stories and looking at books
- Will enjoy finger plays
- Will enjoy action songs
- Will imitate sounds he hears
- Will babble (string consonant and vowels together)
- Will ask for objects by pointing
- Will learn how to point to major body parts when each is named
- Will learn to associate the names of familiar things with their pictures
- Will learn to make the sounds that some animals make
- Will be able to say his own name
- Will be able to say "Mama" and "Dada"
- Will learn to say "bye-bye"
- Will learn to say "thank you"
- Will learn to say "all gone"
- Will have a vocabulary of four to ten words, maybe more

  © Instructional Fair • TS Denison

 General Tips

The drive for toddlers to learn is very powerful. Their learning is in four basic areas: motor (fine and gross), language, cognitive, and social. When one of these four kinds of learning kicks in full gear, the others may take a backseat for awhile. It is as if toddlers need to concentrate on one area at a time. While the first half of the second year is an important motor skills time, learning language will progress from your toddler's own inner excitement. You can enhance your toddler's desire to speak by using some of the following techniques:

Timing—When your child is self-motivated to learn something, she will grasp it quickly. If she is not ready for the concept, it will only frustrate her. So watch for your child's special interest. For example: if you are at a circus and she is excited about watching a clown, that is the perfect time to urge her to say "clown." If your child seems frustrated with a word or concept, forget it for awhile. In a few weeks or a month, she may well be ready to learn it.

Echoing—When a toddler hears sounds and feels free to imitate them, she will practice language development on her own. Encourage your toddler to echo your sounds and words. She will get good practice with correct pronunciation when she imitates what she hears you saying. On the other hand, when you echo your child's words, you let her know that you are listening and that you think her thoughts are important. Echoing works well both ways.

Wait—When your toddler asks for something by pointing, wait a few seconds. Do not jump to her aid. See if she will also give you a word for what she wants. If she gets everything she wants without asking for it, she will not have to learn to speak. This method should only be used if you are sure your toddler knows the word for what she wants. If she does not know the word for what she wants, provide it for her. For example: "Do you want the *book?* Can you say *book?*"

Talk—Have on-going conversations with your toddler. Tell her where you are going, what you are doing, when you will be back. Tell her all about your day. As you work, tell her what you are doing. Invite her to help. Talk about what you see. Recall things you looked at together the previous day. Talk about something that is going to happen in a day or two.

Name—Say the names for the familiar things in your home for your toddler. When you give her a cup of milk, tell her, "Here is your cup of milk." Look at books and magazines and point out familiar objects as you name them.

Listen—When she tries to speak, listen carefully. If you do not understand what she is saying, ask her to point. Reinforce every attempt she makes to communicate verbally with you.

Appropriate toys—Certain toys will help your toddler learn to talk. For developing your toddler's language skills, include board books with simple, colorful pictures or simple stories, and CDs or audiotapes of children's songs.

Language Development Twelve- to Eighteen-Month-Old

Shhhh

Listen, my children, and you shall hear,
Of the midnight ride of Paul Revere...
—Henry Wadsworth Longfellow

Overture

The first step of learning to talk is learning to listen. Reading to your toddler will give her an opportunity to listen to words and see depictions of the words at the same time. Watch your child's face when you read her a book; you will know when she is excited and when she is bored. If she wiggles around and does not want to sit still long enough to look at a book, try a different book or wait for a week or two before trying again.

Performance

Play: Give your child an opportunity to hear stories written especially for toddlers.
What you will need: The board book *Jamberry* by Bruce Degen (Harperfestival, 1995) is about a boy and bear who go romping through berry patches.
How to play: Find a comfortable place. Hold your toddler in your lap so she can see the pictures in the book. Before you open the book, tell her the magic words "Shhh, listen." Whisper for her to listen. Touch her ears. When she is ready to listen, open the book.

Finale

"Boynton on Board" is a series of concept board books that have been described as "baby books with bounce." Written by Sandra Boynton and published by Workman Publishing Group, *Barnyard Dance!* is especially delightful for toddlers. Cartoon animals will no doubt hold your baby's attention. Check your local library for other board books by the same author or different authors your toddler might enjoy.

Traditional Rhymes will provide your baby with the rhythm that turns a story into a song. Appropriate board books of nursery rhymes by Iona Archibald Opie (Candlewick Press) include:
- *Humpty Dumpty: And Other Rhymes*
- *Little Boy Blue: And Other Rhymes*
- *Wee Willie Winkie: And Other Rhymes*
- *Pussycat, Pussycat: And Other Rhymes*

If possible, begin your baby's personal library of board books so she can hear them read again and again. The chubby, sturdy pages will make it possible for your baby to look at the pictures independently.

Encore

Most toddlers cannot sit still long enough or have the concentration to listen to a long story. Toddlers prefer picking out and pointing to pictures in a book or magazine. Board books will offer you short stories with few words and bright pictures to pique your baby's interest. Children this age will sometimes listen to short stories told about familiar objects or people in the family.

© Instructional Fair • TS Denison

This Little Cow

This little cow eats grass,
This little cow eats hay,
This little cow drinks water,
This little cow runs away,
This little cow does nothing,
But lie down all day.

Overture

Many toddlers have played the game "This Little Piggy Went to Market." In China, instead of tweaking toes and calling them little piggies, the rhyme is about cows eating grass and hay.

Performance

Play: To encourage your toddler's language development, use simple finger plays such as "This Little Cow."

What you will need: No special equipment is needed for this game.

How to play: Place your barefoot baby on his back. Tug a little toe as you say each line of the rhyme.

This little cow eats grass, (*Wiggle big toe.*)
This little cow eats hay, (*Wiggle second toe.*)
This little cow drinks water, (*Wiggle middle toe.*)
This little cow runs away, (*Wiggle fourth toe.*)
This little cow does nothing but lie down all day. (*Wiggle little toe.*)

Use the Traditional Rhyme to play with fingers, too.

Finale

Substitute other animals and make silly sounds while you play the game.
For example:
- ◆ This little doggie eats wieners—woof, woof, woof.
- ◆ This little kitty drinks milk—meow, meow, meow.
- ◆ This little birdie eats bread—tweet, tweet, tweet.
- ◆ This little (baby's name) eats cereal—yum, yum, yum.

Encore

Toddlers must put together all kinds of sounds. Games that name familiar objects will help him comprehend the words' meanings. Your child will like the rhythm of Traditional Rhymes and enjoy hearing them over and over.

Language Development **Twelve- to Eighteen-Month-Old**

Three Bears in the Bed

Three bears in the bed, and one bear said,
"I'm crowded. Roll over." So they all rolled over.

Overture

The brain clearly is attuned to language acquisition in the early years. Watch your toddler's face when she is listening to other people. She is sorting and matching words and images in her mind.

Performance

Play: To encourage your toddler to participate in an action song, play "Three Bears in the Bed."
What you will need: Three stuffed toy bears or other stuffed animals
How to play: Place your toddler and bears on a bed. Lay the bears side-by-side touching one another, with one bear right on the edge of the bed. Use the rhyme with actions.

Three bears in the bed, and one bear said, (*Stand up bear farthest from edge.*)
"I'm crowded. Roll over." (*Bounce bear as if it is talking, then lay it down again.*)
So they all rolled over. (*Roll bears so that one falls off the edge.*)
Two bears in the bed, and one bear said, (*Stand up bear farthest from edge.*)
"I'm crowded. Roll over." (*Bounce bear as if it is talking, then lay it down again.*)
So they all rolled over. (*Roll bears so that one falls off the edge.*)
One bear in the bed, and he said, (*Stand up the last bear.*)
"I'm lonely!" (*Bounce bear as if it is talking.*)

Finale

To take the action rhyme one step further, ask your toddler where the other two bears are. Ask her to get them for you. Help her climb down off the bed. Replace the bears and begin again. The game can be played with five or six bears. Or play with other soft toys like three dolls in the bed, or three pillows on the bed, or three balls on the table.

Encore

While using the word "roll" in the action song, show your toddler how it feels to roll. Place her on the floor. With her legs out straight and arms pulled in straight, roll her over several times. Tell her the word "roll" as you are moving her.

© Instructional Fair • TS Denison

Ooooooh

a e i o and YOU!

Overture

There are essential points in time when learning is optimum. Every normal child acquires the elements of his language between the ages of one and four. It is never too soon to stimulate the toddler's language development by playing games that incorporate vowel sounds.

Performance

Play: To give your toddler an opportunity to imitate some long vowel sounds he hears, play "Ooooooh."

What you will need: No special equipment is needed to play this game.

How to play: Place your toddler in your lap where he can see your mouth. Introduce the long vowel sounds: A, E, I, O, and U. Say each one as a long, drawn-out word: Aaaaaaaaaaa. (Pause.) Eeeeeeeeeee. (Pause.) Etc.

Examples:

"A" as in "ape" or "vase"
"E" as in "peek," "eagle," or "bee"
"I" as in "pie," "bike," or "pine"
"O" as in "boat" or "pole"
And "U" as in "you" or "blue"

Finale

Do not combine the vowel sounds with any other letters. Just say them as drawn-out sounds. Your toddler will pay close attention to the way you hold your mouth when you make each sound. After you say each sound, pause to give your toddler a chance to make the sound, too. On other occasions, sit in front of a full-length mirror when making sounds so your toddler can watch your mouth. Sit where toddler can see both your face and his in the mirror at the same time. Make the sound of a long vowel. Pause. Repeat so your toddler can watch how you hold your mouth and tongue while making the sound.

Encore

As your toddler gets older, add a consonant in front of each long vowel to make new sounds. Say the new sounds to your toddler the way you said the long vowels.

Examples:

Ba, Be, Bi, Bo, Bu
Da, De, Di, Do, Du
Fa, Fe, Fi, Fo, Fu

Babble Back at Baby

Tar-baby ain't sayin' nuthin',
Brer Fox, he lay low.
— "Uncle Remus and His Friends"

Overture

Most babies begin to babble at about six months. The babbles sound pretty much the same no matter what country you live in. "Goo-goo," "Mama," and "Dada" are the sounds often heard in countries that speak languages other than English.

Performance

Play: To encourage your baby to babble and begin to speak words, babble back to your baby.
What you will need: No special equipment is needed to play this game.
How to play: Hold your baby in your lap. Wait to hear a sound. Echo the sound you hear. Babble back to your baby. All during the day, listen for any sounds your toddler makes. Babble the sounds back to her.

Finale

When you played "Babble, Babble" (see page 44) with your baby, it was suggested that you make a list of the sounds your baby makes. Use some of these favorite sounds to babble with your baby. Now that your toddler is older, take the game "Babble, Babble" one step further. Besides just echoing the sounds your baby makes, make new ones for her to imitate. Pick simple sounds and use only one or two sounds at a time. Toddlers often babble a consonant followed by a long or short vowel. Try combining a variety of consonants followed by a vowel to make one-syllable sounds.

Encore

Give your toddler a new word each time she experiences a feeling.
Examples:

- Touch a carton of ice cream—say "cold."
- Touch a warm soup bowl—say "warm."
- Touch bath water—say "wet."
- Touch sand—say "dry."
- Touch paper—say "smooth."
- Touch sandpaper—say "rough."
- Touch a kitty—say "soft."
- Touch satin—say "silky."

© Instructional Fair • TS Denison

Name It!

The Queen of Hearts
She made some tarts.
—Traditional Rhyme

Overture

The more personal language is, the more motivated your child will be to learn. For example, when the toddler wants a cookie, he will be more motivated to learn the name of the object because he can see it, hold it, and taste it.

Performance

Play: To encourage your toddler to learn the names of things he points to, play "Name It!"

What you will need: No special equipment is needed to play this game.

How to play: Every time your toddler points to something he wants, name the object three or four times. Emphasize the name of the object.

For example, as he points to a cookie:

◆ Do you want a *cookie?* (He hears the name of what he wants.)
◆ These are good *cookies.* (He hears the name of what he will get.)
◆ Here is your *cookie.* (He hears the name as he touches it.)
◆ Is that a good *cookie?* (He hears the name as he is tasting it.)

Finale

Use pointing as a naming game. Show your toddler how to point to objects and then name each thing he indicates. Take a walk around your house. Let your toddler point to things as you name them. He will think this is a great game because he is controlling what you will name. Also hike around your yard or neighborhood and play the naming game with things found outside.

Encore

During the next few months, your toddler will learn many new words. You can offer him countless opportunities to increase his comprehension vocabulary. Name everything you see him looking at or touching. Play the game in a variety of places including:

◆ When you are riding in the car, point out things and name them.
◆ When you are in the market, point out different foods and name them.
◆ When you walk in the park, point out and name things in nature.

When your toddler can touch the things as you name them, the lesson will become more personal.

Language Development **Twelve- to Eighteen-Month-Old**

Eye Winker

Eye winker,
Nose dropper,
Mouth eater,
Chin chopper,
Chin chopper.
—Traditional Rhyme

Overture

Watch and you will notice that your toddler is interested in her own body parts. She will like learning to name the parts of her body.

Performance

Play: To teach your toddler the names of parts of the face, play "Eye Winker."

What you will need: No special equipment is needed.

How to play: Use a varied version of the rhyme to teach your toddler to point to parts of her face. In the beginning, touch appropriate places on your toddler's face. Then teach her to touch the places you name as you say the rhyme.

Head thinker, (*Touch forehead.*)
Eye winker, (*Touch eyebrows.*)
Nose dropper, (*Touch nose.*)
Mouth eater, (*Touch lips.*)
Chin chopper, (*Chuck chin.*)
Chin chopper. (*Chuck chin again.*)

Finale

Play another face naming game, "Where Is Yours?" Begin by naming a part of the face—"nose." Then point to your nose. Ask your toddler, "Where is your nose?" When she points to her nose, repeat the word "nose." Then point to your eyes and name them. Then ask toddler, "Where are your eyes?" The object is not for her to be able to name the parts of the face; the object of the game is to teach her to point to the place on her face that you name. You can also play "Where Is Yours?" naming basic body parts, including:

◆ Legs, feet, toes
◆ Arms, hands, fingers, thumb
◆ Elbow, knee, shoulder
◆ Head, neck, chest, back, stomach

Encore

When naming parts of the body for your toddler, use the correct terminology. If you want to talk "baby talk" and call her toes "piggies" that is okay when playing games, but using correct names for parts of the body is best when teaching your toddler to speak.

Match Up

Oh, dear! What can the picture be?
Is it a frog, a fly, or a bumble bee?
—Traditional Rhyme

Overture...

During this developmental stage, playing games of labeling and identifying objects will advance your toddler's language development tremendously. He does not have to name the things he sees; just hearing the names and learning to listen will increase his comprehension vocabulary.

Performance...

Play: To encourage your toddler to learn the names of some interesting things that he does not see every day, play "Match Up."
What you will need: From old magazines, cut pictures of interesting objects. Glue each one to an index card.
How to play: Hold your toddler in your lap and show him each picture. Name the object as your toddler looks at, points to, or holds the card. Work on six to ten pictures for several sessions. Then cut out new pictures and make additional cards. Let your child play with the cards independently.

Finale...

Use the cards you create to play guessing games. Place two cards on a table and name one of the pictures. Your toddler is to point to the picture named. When this game gets really easy, place three cards on the table and let your toddler choose each one you name. When your toddler chooses an incorrect card, do not tell him he is wrong. Just name the picture on his card, and place it back on the table. Repeat the name again. This gives him an opportunity to get it right. Praise all efforts playing this game.

Encore ....

Create cards with themes and present the theme cards together. You may choose to make and present a group of picture cards with one of these themes:

◆ People (baby, boy, girl, man, woman)
◆ Farm animals
◆ Zoo animals
◆ Occupations
◆ Clothing items
◆ Toys

When you finish playing with a group of cards, allow the toddler to play with the cards independently.

Language Development Twelve- to Eighteen-Month-Old

Old MacDonald Had a Farm

Old MacDonald had a farm,
E-I-E-I-O!
—Traditional Rhyme

Overture

Listen and you will hear many sounds coming from your toddler. He may try to sing and hum. All the sounds he makes will be more spontaneous now. Toddlers begin to demonstrate a wide range in tone, pitch, and intensity of voice. Watch and you will see your toddler is acutely aware of sounds like bells ringing, whistles blowing, and clocks chiming. Making animal sounds is a favorite game for many toddlers.

Performance

Play: To encourage your toddler's language development, use songs with nonsense sounds such as "Old MacDonald Had a Farm."

What you will need: No special equipment is needed to play this game.

How to play: Sing a different verse of the song every day; each time introduce a new animal sound. Example:

Old MacDonald had a farm, E-I-E-I-O.
And on his farm he had a duck. E-I-E-I-O.
With a quack, quack, here, and a quack, quack, there.
Here a quack, there a quack, everywhere a quack, quack,
Old MacDonald had a farm, E-I-E-I-O.

Have your toddler try to make the quacking sound. After he learns the quacking sound, pause in the verse so he can join in the singing of the song.

Finale

Animals sounds that some toddlers can make include:

◆ Dog—woof, woof
◆ Kitty—purr, purr
◆ Mouse—squeak, squeak
◆ Pig—snort, snort
◆ Chick—peep, peep
◆ Lamb—baa, baa

Encore

Toddlers enjoy hearing repetitive songs and familiar rhymes incorporated with interesting sounds. CDs and audiotapes of rhythmic folk songs and repetitive nursery rhymes are appropriate for toddlers. Hearing inflections and word phrases will prepare your toddler for speaking.

© Instructional Fair • TS Denison

Heeeere's Baby

Bessy Bell and Mary Gray,
Were two bonny lasses.
—Traditional Rhyme

Overture

There is a tremendous variance in the age at which children begin to say recognizable words. Some have a vocabulary of several words by their first birthday; others do not speak until they are two; still others may not speak until they are three. Watch your toddler learning language, the more recognition you give her for speaking, the more stimulated she will be to talk. One of the first words many toddlers learn is her own name.

Performance

Play: To help your toddler learn how to say her name, play "Heeeere's Baby."

What you will need: Hand mirror

How to play: Sit with your toddler in your lap. Ask her, "What is your name?" Then tell her, "Your name is (baby's name)." Ask her if she wants to see (baby's name). Then hold the hand mirror so she can see her own face. Say, "Here's (baby's name). Isn't she beautiful?" Say hello to your toddler's reflection in the mirror. Use her name in the greeting. Ask her, "What is your name?" Play with the mirror and try to get your toddler to say her name.

Finale

Use your toddler's name many times each day. When talking to her siblings, family, and friends, say to your toddler, "Tell them your name." (Do not put her on the spot when she meets the person if she cannot say her name yet. Let her practice with the family first.) To play a game that will provide your toddler a chance to hear her name, play "Peekaboo, Here's Baby." Place the toddler on the floor on her back, facing toward you. Lift both her legs together and sit so her feet conceal her face. Then say "Here's (name)." Open her legs wide so you can see her face. Then bring her feet back together again so you cannot see her face. Repeat.

Encore

Look at photographs of the family. Name each member. When you see photographs of your toddler, point and say her name. Ask her to point to (baby's name). When she can say her name, have her find her face in the photographs, point, and say her name.

"Mama or Dada?"

My mama, and your mama,
Went over the way.
Said my mama, to your mama,
"It's a chop-a-nose day."
—Traditional Rhyme

Overture

When your toddler begins to say a few words, you may find yourself using less "baby talk." Giving the correct pronunciation for words will make learning language easier for your toddler.

Performance

Play: To give your toddler an opportunity to say "mama" or "dada" (or what ever pet names your toddler uses for parents), play "Mama or Dada?"
What you will need: A variety of photographs the toddler's parents
How to play: Seat your toddler on the floor. Place photographs of both parents on the floor between your toddler and you. Hold up a photograph of yourself, and using the pet names your toddler uses to indicate each parent, ask "Mama or Dada?" Then tell your toddler who it is. "It is Mama." Then hold up a photograph of the father and ask "Mama or Dada?" Continue holding up photographs. If your toddler cannot say "Mama" and "Dada" yet, identify each one for your child.

Finale

When your toddler can say his name and say "mama," play "Who Am I?" Ask him, "Who Am I?" When he says "Mama," ask, "Who are you?" Keep asking him in random order questions that can be answered by the toddler's name or "mama."

- ◆ Who sleeps here?
- ◆ Whose shoes are these?
- ◆ Who drives the car?
- ◆ Who is little and beautiful?

Encore

When your child can say "mama" and "dada," give directions including his name for you.
Examples:

- ◆ Mama is going to put you to bed now.
- ◆ Dada is going to give you your bath.
- ◆ Dada is leaving for work now; he will be home later.
- ◆ Mama is going to read a book while (toddler's name) takes a nap.

© Instructional Fair • TS Denison

"Bye-Bye"

Bye-bye, don't cry.
I'll be back by and by.

Overture

Watch your toddler's eyes when some-one leaves the room. One of the first gestures toddlers learn when communicating is to wave "bye-bye." It seems to make the parting sweeter if the child can usher the person away with a wave and a parting word.

Performance

Play: To offer your toddler an opportunity to wave and say "bye-bye," play "Bye-Bye."

What you will need: No special equipment is needed to play this game.

How to play: Hold your toddler in your arms. Walk around the house and wave and say "bye-bye" to objects. Name each object. For example: When leaving the kitchen, wave and say "bye-bye, table." Go into each room and point to three objects as you name each one. Then as you leave that room, wave and say "bye-bye" to each object. "Bye-bye, bed; bye-bye, books; Bye-bye, teddy bear."

Finale

Play "Bye-bye, Ball." Seat your toddler on the floor facing you. Roll a beach ball back and forth between you. Each time you roll the ball away say, "Bye-bye, ball." Soon your toddler will be telling the ball "bye-bye" when she rolls it back to you.

Encore

Walk around your yard and wave and say "bye-bye" to objects including:
- ◆ Bye-bye, tree.
- ◆ Bye-bye, flower.
- ◆ Bye-bye, door.

When Father or Mother leaves for work, siblings leave for school, or friends leave your home, take your toddler outside or to a window where she can see the person leaving. Give the toddler time to wave and shout "bye-bye."

"Thank You"

I thank you for your voices, thank you,
Your most sweet voices.
—William Shakespeare

Overture

Your toddler's vocabulary may consist of several sounds that he makes consistently to mean certain objects. "Ba" might be his word for *bottle*. "Gog" might be his way of saying *dog*. When you hear sounds repeated daily, you will know these are his first words. During this developmental stage, he will begin to use sounds to mean words.

Performance

Play: Encourage your toddler to be grateful by playing "Thank You."
What you will need: Two small, paper shopping bags with handles; a variety of toys
How to play: Seat the toddler on the floor. Place toys on the floor between your toddler and you. Ask the toddler for a toy, then place it in a bag and say, "Thank you." Hand him a toy. Help him put it in his bag. Say, "Thank you." Repeat putting toys in the bags and saying "Thank you." When all the toys have been put in the bags, pour them out and begin again.

Finale

Your toddler's word for "thank you" might be "ke ku" or "tank to," or another variation. It does not matter how he pronounces the words. The important thing is to teach him to verbalize his gratefulness. When you give him things, say, "Thank you" so he hears the words. After he learns the words, when you give him something, you may even ask, "What do you say?" and wait for a "thank you."

Encore

"Please" can also be used to play a game. When you ask for a toy, say, "Please." Again, your toddler's word for "please" may be an abbreviated one. Using "please" and "thank you" during the day will be the quickest way for your toddler to learn good manners.

  © Instructional Fair • TS Denison

"All Gone"

Fill it up.
Pour it out.
All gone!

Overture

"All gone" may be among your toddler's first two-word phrases. One reason toddlers learn this expression so quickly is because many mothers use the phrase when a baby finishes a bottle or bowl of cereal. The words are easy to say, which may also be a reason toddlers learn the phrase quickly.

Performance

Play: To help your toddler practice saying the phrase, play "All Gone!"

What you will need: Tub of sand (or rice); small, plastic pitcher; scoops and small measuring cups

How to play: Seat your toddler on the floor. Place the tub of sand (or rice) and pitcher on the floor between you and your toddler. Fill the pitcher with sand. Then slowly pour it out. When the pitcher is empty, turn it upside down, hold it up so your toddler can see it is empty and say, "All gone." Then fill it up with sand again. Have your toddler help you fill it with sand. When it is full, slowly pour out the sand. Hold the pitcher upside down again. Show your toddler it is empty once again. Give her time to say "All gone." Repeat until your toddler is helping you exclaim, "All gone!"

Finale

Turn this into a guessing game. Fill the pitcher with sand. Pour out part of the sand and ask, "All gone?" Keep pouring out the sand and asking if it is "all gone." You can answer for the toddler. "No, it is not all gone." Then when it is empty, let the toddler respond.

Encore

Use the phrase during the day when your toddler is performing normal tasks including:
- ◆ When your toddler finishes her bottle, say, "All gone."
- ◆ When she finishes her cereal, say, "All gone."
- ◆ When letting the water out of the bath and it has drained completely, say, "All gone."

"All done," is another two-word phrase toddlers learn early on. After a bath or meal say, "All done." Perhaps when your toddler is eating or bathing, ask, "All done?"

Language Development Twelve- to Eighteen-Month-Old

Time to Talk

"The time has come," the Walrus said,
"To talk of many things:
Of shoes—and ships—and sealing wax—
Of cabbages—and kings—and why the sea is boiling hot—
And whether pigs have wings."
—Lewis Carroll

Overture

Between one and one-half years of age, toddlers vary in the number of words they can speak. Some only speak babbles; others will speak a few basic words. If your toddler is making giant leaps in fine and gross motor skills, his language may be developing a bit more slowly. If, however, he is concentrating on learning language, it may seem he is not learning many new motor skills. Remember, toddlers concentrate on one basic learning area at a time.

Performance

Play: To encourage your toddler to use his four- to ten-word vocabulary, play "Time to Talk."
What you will need: Make a list of the words that your toddler can speak. The "words" may be babbling sounds that are used consistently to mean certain things.
How to play: Use your toddler's words. Pause so he can converse with you by repeating them. Have conversations that include all of his words every day. As he learns new words, add them to the list.

Finale

Write the words your toddler knows on index cards, then place them around the house for other family members to read. Urge everyone to use your toddler's words in conversations with him.

Encore

Remember, your toddler is basically learning language from what he hears you and others in the family say. Give your toddler the consideration you would want those in a foreign country to give you, if you were learning a new language.
- ◆ Slow down your speech.
- ◆ Enunciate.
- ◆ Use inflection in your voice.
- ◆ Sing songs with familiar words.
- ◆ Point at objects and name them.

© Instructional Fair • TS Denison

Keeping Track

Milestone	Date	Comments
Can listen to short stories		
Can sit still to look at pictures in books		
Enjoys finger plays		
Enjoys action songs		
Can imitate sounds that are heard		
Babbles strings of sounds		
Can ask for things by pointing		
Can point to body parts that are named		
Can match pictures with their names		
Can make sounds of some animals		
Can say his/her own name		
Can say words for mother and father		
Can say "bye-bye"		
Can say "thank you"		
Can say "all gone"		
Can say four to ten words		

Copy Cat

Cognitive Development

Contemplate

In the next six months your toddler will become upright and walk most of the time. His discoveries will no longer be limited by his crawling range and his low-to-the-ground perspective. His curiosity will know no bounds. His cognitive development will be a natural result of his experimentation with everything he sees, hears, touches, smells, and tastes. Basically, your toddler will learn through four different channels:

◆ **Pleasure**—Rewarding experiences
◆ **Imitation**—Copying rewarded behaviors of adults and other children
◆ **Participation**—Playing with others or by himself
◆ **Communications**—Being with others and seeing what gets their attention and praise

In-depth tips about using these four learning channels to increase your toddler's cognitive skills are found on the following page.

Cognitive Milestones: Twelve to Eighteen Months

◆ Will be able to imitate many kinds of actions
◆ Will combine objects with other objects to create new ways of doing things
◆ Will use the trial-and-error method to discover new solutions to problems
◆ Can retrieve a hidden toy
◆ Can hide a toy for another person to find
◆ Will look up and down on command
◆ Will scribble on paper, holding the crayon in a fist
◆ Will imitate sounds like cough, nose blowing, and sneezing
◆ Will begin to understand accomplishments and look for praise
◆ Will begin to be able to play alone for short periods of time
◆ Will search for a missing parent who is in the house
◆ Will understand "push," "pull," and "lift"
◆ Will learn how to blow bubbles
◆ Will pick up things to smell them

© Instructional Fair • TS Denison

General Tips

Learning is so much fun for toddlers that they are naturally motivated by the *pleasurable process*. Cuddling a soft toy is comforting. Poking at buttons that make music is stimulating. Batting at a ball with a hand and changing its direction is empowering. Hiding in a cardboard box is exciting. From dawn until dusk your toddler will be busy learning through her play.

It has been said that *imitation* is the greatest form of flattery. When it comes to toddlers, imitating is not only their way of telling others how special they are, it is their way of learning what is expected of them and what is required to be part of a family. Giving your toddler tasks to help you in the house so she can imitate your work will bring her the feelings of both satisfaction and belonging.

With each new fine and gross motor skill your toddler learns, new games will become available to her. Her *participation* will only be limited by her ability. The more willing to participate a child is, the more she will learn from any experience. Involving the five senses in activities will engage your child at many different levels. Play games that include songs, movement, looking, smelling, and tasting.

If pleasure, imitation, and participation are the "meat and potatoes" of learning, *communication* is the "dessert." Human beings live in their conversations. Up until now, your toddler has not really been able to be very verbal with you, but in her exchanges of crying, smiling, cooing, and pointing, she has let you know what she wanted and did not want. Now your baby will begin to be more and more interested in exploring the effects she has on you and other people. What works best for getting attention? Showing off? Shouting? Hugging? Now is a perfect time to teach your toddler simple rules. Use your child's desire for attention and need for approval to communicate what you need and expect from her. For a toddler to learn rules, there must be only a few and they should involve important things like her safety and well-being. When disciplining your toddler keep in mind these rules:

◆ Ignore the things she does that you do not like—give her absolutely no recognition for them.
◆ Praise and appreciate the things she does that are appropriate and positive.

Cognitive Development Twelve- to Eighteen-Month-Old

How Do You Do?

How do you do?"
And "How do you do?"
And "How do you do?" again.
                    —Traditional Rhyme

Overture

During this developmental stage, imitation will be a big part of your toddler's learning. It will no longer be enough to look at things, he will want to touch everything he sees and use objects in the appropriate ways.

Performance

Play: To encourage your toddler to imitate the actions such as shaking hands when meeting people, play "How Do You Do?"
What you will need: No special equipment is needed to play this game.
How to play: Use the Traditional Rhyme as an action song.

One misty, moisty morning, (*Wrap arms around body as if cold.*)
When cloudy was the weather, (*Look to the clouds.*)
I chanced to meet an old man, clothed all in leather. (*Use hand in sweeping motion to indicate clothing.*)
He began to compliment, (*Nod.*)
And I began to grin. (*Smile.*)
"How do you do?" (*Shake hands with toddler.*)
And "How do you do?" (*Continue shaking hands with toddler.*)
And "How do you do?" again! (*Continue shaking hands with toddler.*)

Finale

Use another rhyme to play a shaking hands game, too.
Example:

Doctor Foster went to Gloucester, (*March in place.*)
In a shower of rain. (*Cover head with hands.*)
He stepped in a puddle, (*Pretend to step in a puddle.*)
Right up to his middle, (*Pretend to be very wet.*)
And he never went there again. (*Shake hands and walk away.*)

Encore

Use the last three lines of the first rhyme (the shaking hands part) as a game when you first see your toddler in the morning, after a nap, when coming home from shopping, etc. When your toddler meets new people, if he enjoys shaking hands as a greeting, encourage him to do so.

© Instructional Fair • TS Denison

Building Bridges

The youth gets together his materials to build a bridge to the moon. . . .
—Henry David Thoreau

Overture

Watch your toddler and you will see her using the most powerful tool for learning—*play*. Learning is not memorizing facts. It is a period for playing with ideas, building self-confidence, and taking materials and combining them in interesting ways.

Performance

Play: Give your toddler an opportunity to combine toys and sand to create new ways of playing.
What you will need: Sandbox or tub of sand, wooden blocks, cardboard strips
How to play: Demonstrate how to use the cardboard and wooden blocks to build a simple bridge. (Block at either end, cardboard on top.) Encourage any combination of cardboard and wooden blocks that your toddler creates. Build a bridge with the blocks and cardboard in the sandbox. Line up wooden blocks to make a "train."

Finale

At 12 to 15 months, toddlers may begin to use combinations of objects for play. Give your toddler different combinations of toys for her to use:
- Wooden blocks and small sheets of cardboard
- Shoe boxes (with "doors" and "windows" cut in them) and little plastic people
- Shoelaces and large wooden beads (with adult supervision)
- Paper plates, cups, and place mats
- Hats and plastic hand mirror
- Metal cars and cardboard ramps

Encore

Give your toddler the opportunity to play in a plastic tub of water. Provide wooden blocks and plastic toys. Demonstrate how the toys float in the water. Do the wooden blocks float? Do the plastic toys float? Place wooden blocks on top of a sheet of plastic and see if it will still float. Pile more blocks on top. Allow your toddler free play and time to experiment with the water and buoyant toys. On other occasions give your toddler a tub of sand, a tub of water, wooden blocks, and plastic toys. Watch to see how she combines these materials for play.

Does It Fit?

> *. . . seeks a little thing to do,*
> *Sees it and does it.*
>
> —Robert Browning

Overture..

Toddlers have an awkward grasp. Games that encourage your toddler to grasp and let go, push and poke, will help him develop skills needed to experiment with sizes and shapes of objects.

Performance...

Play: To encourage your toddler to use a trial-and-error method to discover new solutions to problems, play "Does It Fit?"

What you will need: Large coffee can with a plastic lid, bowl, pebbles 2"–4" (51–102 mm) in diameter

How to play: Cut a hole in the lid of the can 2"–3" (51–76 mm) in diameter. Place the bowl of pebbles on the floor between you and your toddler. Show him how to fit each pebble into the can through the hole. Ask him, "Does it fit?" Let your toddler experiment with the pebbles to see which ones will slip through the hole and which ones will not fit. Each time he tries to fit a pebble into the hole in the lid, ask, "Does it fit?"

Finale ....

Cut a square hole in the lid of another coffee can. The hole should be only slightly bigger than your toddler's wooden blocks. Show him how to put the blocks into the can through the hole. It is best if the blocks have to be turned in a certain way to slide into the hole. Give your toddler plenty of free time with this fitting game.

Encore ....

By age one-and-a-half, many toddlers are interested in simple puzzles. Puzzles for toddlers should have only three or four whole shape pieces with little knobs for holding them. Thick plastic pieces with rounded edges are most useful because they are washable and too big to put in your toddler's mouth.

© Instructional Fair • TS Denison

Go-Seek

To strive, to seek, to find. . . .
—Alfred Lord Tennyson

Overture

Toddlers from 12 to 18 months of age are very interested in operating mechanisms, looking for hidden objects, fitting things into other things, putting pieces together, and taking things apart. Watch your toddler as she learns to open lids or doors and manipulate dials, switches, and knobs. You will see her confidence growing in leaps and bounds. Each new accomplishment will empower her.

Performance

Play: To encourage your toddler to retrieve a hidden toy, play "Go-Seek."
What you will need: A large stuffed animal
How to play: Have your toddler close her eyes as you hide the stuffed animal. Leave a bit of it exposed so she can see it. Tell her to open her eyes and "Go-Seek." Verbally praise your toddler when she finds the animal. Each time have her close her eyes while you hide the animal. Repeat until she is no longer interested in playing the game.

Finale

For a more sedate hiding game, play "Seek on Me." Hold your toddler in your lap. Ask her to close her eyes. Hide a small ball in one hand, in a pocket, under your hat, on your head, etc. Tell your child to open her eyes and say, "Seek on me." When she finds the ball, act very surprised. Repeat by hiding the ball in yet another conspicuous place. This game can be played while waiting in a doctor's office, in line at the supermarket, etc. On another occasion go into your toddler's bedroom. Pick up a toy and show it to her. Then have her close her eyes. Place the toy with the other toys. When she opens her eyes ask her to remember which toy was hidden and pick it up. This kind of game will help your toddler develop good visual memory.

Encore

Hide-and-seek games are good tests of *object permanency*. Point out things that can be viewed day after day, such as a particular tree in the yard, the bird feeder, and so on. Then when you are out and about ask questions like:

- ◆ Where is the big tree?
- ◆ Where is the bird feeder?
- ◆ Where is our car?

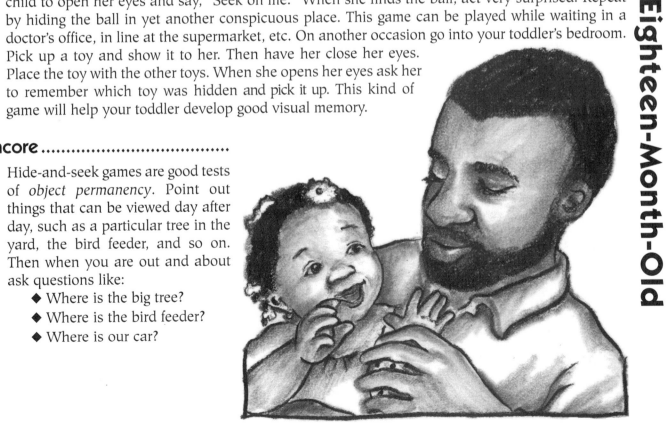

Go-Hide

In the calm region where no night
Can hide us from each other's sight.

—Henry King

Overture

Symbolic play starts early in the second year. Your toddler will like to pretend he is daddy or someone else. Watch him playing with a doll; he may treat it as though it is a real baby. Watch him playing with a truck; he will "drive" it back and forth. Most of all he will enjoy games shared with others, but he is old enough now to begin spending time playing alone.

Performance

Play: To encourage your toddler to hide a toy for you to find, play "Go-Hide."

What you will need: No special equipment is needed to play this game.

How to play: After your toddler knows how to play "Go-Seek," he is ready to learn how to play "Go-Hide." Instead of searching for a hidden object, have your toddler hide and you will search for him. It may be difficult at first to get your toddler to understand the reverse process. But once he catches on to this game, he will be eager to "go-hide." It may be impossible for him to hide quietly because the excitement of the game is sure to get giggles and squeals as he waits to be found.

Finale

Using a toy, play another hide-and-seek game. Give your toddler a toy and close your eyes. Tell him to hide the toy. In the beginning he may not even try to conceal it. He will place it somewhere in plain sight. Look around and pretend not to see the toy for awhile. As you walk around looking for it, his delight will grow as you get closer and closer to the toy. When you find the toy, tell him how special the hiding place was. Then give him the toy. Close your eyes and let him hide it again.

Encore

When you play hide-and-seek games, it is the perfect time to use such words as: "in," "under," "behind," "on," etc. For example, when you find a teddy bear behind the sofa, verbalize this to your toddler. "Very good. You hid the teddy bear *behind* the sofa." When giving your toddler hints to find a hidden object, say something like this: "If you stand in front of the television, you will be able to see the teddy bear." Or, "If you look *under* the chair, you will find the bear."

Look Up

Look up; look down;
Look around; you're a clown.

Overture

Watch how your toddler observes the world, and you will see her growing awareness. She will constantly be watching what is happening. She will keep one eye on you and one on her toys. When new people enter the picture, she will be aware of their presence and eager to get their attention. Getting her to look in particular directions will be fun and sometimes challenging. As any parent who has taken a child for a professional photograph will tell you, when it comes to where to focus, a toddler has a mind of her own.

Performance

Play: To help your toddler understand the directions "up," "down," and "around," play "Look Up!"
What you will need: A small interesting object like a colorful pinwheel or a soft toy
How to play: Place the child in a sitting position. Stand in front of her. Hold the toy above her head and say, "Look up." Praise her when she tips her head back and looks up. Say "Up" again. Then put the toy on the floor where she can see it. Say, "Look down." When she bows her head and focuses on the toy on the floor, praise her. Repeat the word "down." Then move the toy around her head at eye level. Say, "Look around." Repeat several times as she moves her head to follow the toy. Repeat the game, quickening the pace and using a different toy each time.

Finale

After playing this game of focusing with a toy, try the game without a toy. Try to get her to move her head and eyes in the appropriate direction without something on which to focus. Use your own eyes and head to show her how to look "up," "down," and "all around." Use the rhyme as an action play.
Example:
Look up; (*Tip head and look up at the ceiling.*)
Look down; (*Bow head and look at the floor.*)
Look around; (*Look to the right; look to the left.*)
You're a clown. (*Big smile!*)

Encore

Use the position words "up," "down," and "around" on outings.
- Look *up* and see the clouds.
- Look *down* and see the grass.
- Look *around* and see the people.

Cognitive Development **Twelve- to Eighteen-Month-Old**

Doodle, Doodle

Doodle, doodle, doo.
Red, yellow, blue.

Overture

Watch a toddler coloring with a crayon and most likely he will be holding the crayon in his fist. He will not have the dexterity to hold the crayon in a writing position for many months.

Performance

Play: To give your toddler his first opportunity to doodle on paper, play "Doodle, Doodle."
What you will need: Primary color crayons (red, blue, and yellow), large sheet of paper
How to play: Seat your toddler in a high chair so his tray will serve as his desk. Place the paper on his tray. Give him one crayon. Show him how to draw a scribble with the crayon. Scribble on the page with him. Praise his every effort to create lines on the page. Date his first work of art and frame it or put it away in a safe place. A notebook of unlined paper will work well for his scribbles during the next few months. Save his first book of artistic works.

Finale

Cherishing your toddler's artwork will send a clear message to him regarding its value. When your toddler scribbles, hang his work on the refrigerator, frame it and hang it on a wall, put it in a scrapbook, etc. Papers he scribbles can also be used to wrap gifts, make stationery to send out-of-town family members, or used as place mats (covered with clear adhesive-backed plastic) at a special meal.

Encore

You can increase your toddler's desire to be creative by doing or not doing certain things including:

- Provide paper and crayons so he can scribble at will.
- Provide a place where he can work comfortably.
- Do not label the scribbles he draws as objects.
- Encourage him to create wonderful scribbles.
- Praise him for the powerful lines and squiggles he can make.
- Do not draw simple shapes or objects on his paper; instead, stay with the spirit of scribbling.

  © Instructional Fair • TS Denison

Excuuuuse Me!

Sneeze on Monday, sneeze for danger.
Sneeze on Tuesday, kiss a stranger.
Sneeze on Wednesday, receive a letter.
Sneeze on Thursday, something better.
Sneeze on Friday, expect sorrow.
Sneeze on Saturday, joy tomorrow.
—Traditional Rhyme

Overture

Watch, and you will notice that your toddler imitates the sounds she hears around her. She may find it amusing that unexpected sounds sneak out of her mouth like sneezes, hiccups, coughs, giggles, and burps.

Performance

Play: To help your toddler imitate sounds she hears, play "Excuuuuse Me!"
What you will need: No special equipment is needed to play this game.
How to play: Seat your toddler in your lap where she can see your face. One at a time, make sounds, such as a cough, nose blowing, giggle, hiccup, or sneeze. Follow each sound with the phrase "Excuse me." Encourage your toddler to imitate the sounds and say "Excuse me." The phrase might turn out to be more like "Squz me" and that is okay. Just have fun with this activity.

Finale

Your toddler will be very interested in the sounds you can make with your mouth, lips, tongue, etc. Make lots of interesting sounds for her to hear:

- ◆ Whistle
- ◆ Click the tongue
- ◆ Blow air through closed lips
- ◆ Blow air under extended tongue
- ◆ Kiss
- ◆ Open and close lips rapidly

Encore

It is never too early to teach your child good manners. As soon as she begins to talk, she should be encouraged to say "please," "thank you," and "excuse me." The more you use these words, the more she will hear them. Teaching your toddler to cover her nose when she sneezes or her mouth when she coughs can also be part of her early training. If taught early on, these actions will become like reflexes to her. The only way children can learn manners is by watching others. She will not learn how to do what you *say* as quickly as she will learn how to do what you *do*.

Cognitive Development Twelve- to Eighteen-Month-Old

Good for You!

Hop away, skip away, my baby wants to play;
My baby wants to play every day.
—Traditional Rhyme

Overture

Watch your toddler playing, and you may notice that he will often look to you for praise. With his eyes he will search your face for approval. He not only wants to master new tasks, he wants you to acknowledge his learning.

Performance

Play: To celebrate his accomplishments and lavish him with praise, play "Good for You!"
What you will need: Assortment of toys: ball, doll, blocks
How to play: Place the toys on the floor between your and your toddler. As he plays, tell him "Good for you!"

- ◆ If he rolls a ball, say "Good for you; you can roll a ball."
- ◆ If he holds the doll, say "Good for you; you are holding your dolly."
- ◆ If he stacks blocks, say "Good for you; you know how to stack the blocks."

Acknowledge your toddler's accomplishments not only with praise but by naming the skill he has mastered. That way he is hearing the words for his actions: roll, hold, stack, etc.

Finale

When you praise your toddler, watch his face. Which compliments make him the happiest? Just like big people, toddlers have special feelings about themselves. Try a varied approach to your compliments to see which ones your toddler likes best:

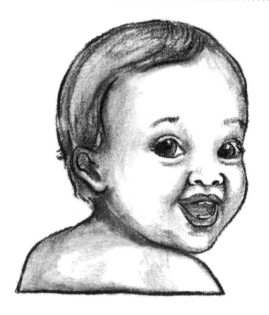

- ◆ Big boy! (girl)
- ◆ I love watching you play.
- ◆ You have good ideas for using your toys.
- ◆ I like how creative you are with the blocks.
- ◆ I like how coordinated you are playing with the ball.
- ◆ I can see how smart you are working with that puzzle.
- ◆ You make me happy when we are together.
- ◆ I feel very proud of you.

Encore

When you see your toddler looking to you for praise, it is important that he hears it immediately. Even a smile says "Good for you." If his plea to be recognized is ignored, he may go to greater and greater lengths to get your attention. When toddlers cannot get attention for good behavior, they sometimes turn to negative behavior.

            © Instructional Fair • TS Denison

By Yourself

When I was a bachelor, I lived by myself,
And all the bread and cheese I got I put upon a shelf.
The rats and the mice did lead me such a life,
That I went to market, to get myself a wife.
—Traditional Rhyme

Overture

Your toddler may become more demanding of your time. She will especially enjoy playing when she has an adult or older sibling with her. To foster her ability to play alone, you may need to verbally guide her from activity to activity.

Performance

Play: To encourage your toddler to play by herself at times, play "By Yourself."
What you will need: Play area where your toddler has access to all of her toys
How to play: Place your toddler in her room or place where she has a number of toys. While working in a nearby room, talk to her so she knows you are nearby. Tell her "You can play by yourself." Interact with her games with conversation from another room. When she demands your attention, explain that you are busy but give her another idea for her next game.
Examples:
- ◆ Rock your dolly, feed her, and put her to bed.
- ◆ Have you played with your puzzles yet? Get out your new puzzle.
- ◆ Build something with your blocks. Can you stack some blocks and knock them down?
- ◆ Look at your books. Find the pictures of the dog and cat.

Finale

Every day for a week, have 10-minute play-by-yourself periods. The next week, extend the daily sessions to 15 minutes. After a few months your toddler might be able to play on her own for an hour or longer at a stretch. Praise your toddler for her ability to play alone. You might say something like this: "You are getting very big. When you can play all by yourself, I know you are getting to be a big girl."

Encore

Having a place where your toddler can play in each room will help keep her entertained while you work on a project. If she refuses to play away from you, a box of toys that can be moved from room to room will help her amuse herself for periods of time. In the beginning, she may only be able to play alone for short periods without wanting your attention. Help her extend her solitary play periods a little each day. Teaching her to be independent and meet her own needs will help her grow to be a self-sufficient, healthy adult.

Here I Am

Here I am,
Ready or not!

Overture

Although your toddler will begin to play alone and not need constant attention, he will still keep constant vigilance regarding your whereabouts. Hearing you talking on the telephone in your bedroom, banging pots and pans in the kitchen, or key stroking on your computer will be comforting to him.

Performance

Play: To encourage your toddler to search for a missing parent who is in the house, play "Here I Am."
What you will need: No special equipment is needed to play this game.
How to play: Play this game like "Hide-and-Seek." Give verbal cues about your whereabouts. Have your toddler sit on a sofa or child-sized chair while you hide somewhere in the house. Then call to your child, "Here I am." Each time he calls to you in his search reply, "Here I am." As your toddler listens to the sound of your voice, he will be able to identify your whereabouts.

Finale

Play another version of this game. Instead of just saying "Here I am," give clues to your child regarding your whereabouts. Examples:
- Come look in my bedroom. I am behind the chair in my bedroom.
- Come look in the kitchen. I am under the table in the kitchen.
- Come look in your bedroom. I am in the closet in your bedroom.

Encore

After your toddler can walk, encourage him to do things on his own with simple instructions from you. For example, if he wants his ball, tell him to get it. Explain where it is and say "Go get it." Challenge him with other simple tasks.
Examples:
- Will you please put this ball in the toy box in your bedroom?
- Will you please get me the cup that is on the table?
- Please put this newspaper on the table in the living room.
- Please take this bowl to the kitchen and put it in the sink.

Push, Pull, Lift

Tit, tat, toe, my first go.
Three jolly butcher boys all in a row.
Stick one up,
Stick one down,
Stick one on the old man's crown.
—Traditional Rhyme

Overture

Watch your toddler at play, and you will see that she probably enjoys practicing all of her emerging skills. She will explore an object to discover its shape and weight by pushing, pulling, and lifting.

Performance

Play: To give your toddler opportunities to practice emerging skills, play "Push, Pull, Lift."

What you will need: Child-size broom, regular-size broom

How to play: Give your toddler her broom. Hold your own broom. Then give verbal commands and demonstrate each movement:

- ◆ **Push**—Hold the handle and push the broom in front of you across the floor.
- ◆ **Pull**—Hold the handle and pull the broom behind you.
- ◆ **Lift**—Holding the broom handle with both hands far apart, lift the broom like a barbell, up and over the head and then back down again.

Progress to playing the game at a quicker pace with music, like a little dance: push, pull, lift, lift, push, pull, lift, lift, etc.

Finale

Use the rhyme as an action song to play games with the brooms.
Example:

Tit, tat, toe, my first go. (*Push the broom.*)
Three jolly butcher boys all in a row. (*Pull the broom.*)
Stick one up, (*Lift broom up.*)
Stick one down, (*Lower broom down.*)
Stick one on the old man's crown. (*Lift broom to rest on top of head.*)

Encore

Toddlers especially enjoy pulling things around. Create a train with cardboard boxes and clothesline. Poke small holes in the boxes and attach 10-inch (25-cm) lengths of clothesline between the boxes. Push the rope through the small hole in each box, then tie a big knot in the rope inside the box to keep it from slipping out. Attach two, three, or even four boxes together. Finally, tie a 2 ft. (61 cm) rope to the front of the train so your toddler can pull it. Let your toddler help you decorate the train using markers to draw and color shapes. On other occasions, tie different objects to a rope, including egg cartons, shoe boxes, etc., and let your toddler pull them around. The sense of power that drives your toddler to push and pull will also make her want to lift and carry heavy objects. When she lifts heavy items it will make her feel strong and powerful.

Cognitive Development Twelve- to Eighteen-Month-Old

Pick One, Any One

Pickeleem, pickleem, pummis-stone!
What is the news, my beautiful one?
—Traditional Rhyme

Overture

Watch your toddler looking at something, and you will see how his concentration is better than ever before. As he gets closer to 18 months of age, he will be able to keep his mind focused for even longer periods of time.

Performance

Play: To encourage your toddler to remember where things are hidden, play "Pick One, Any One."

What you will need: Two identical plastic bowls turned upside down, a small rubber ball

How to play: Place the ball under one of the bowls. Let your toddler watch you putting the ball under the bowl. Then ask him to point to the bowl that is covering the ball. Play the game very simply for a while. After a while, add the element of mixing the bowls up a little after placing the ball under one. With a hand on each bowl, slowly move them around each other. Then let your toddler try to pick out the bowl where the ball is hidden. When he points to the wrong bowl, lift it up and show him that the ball is not there. Then let him point to the other bowl. Pick up that bowl and say, "You are right! Here it is." Always be very positive about the games you play with your toddler. There is no right or wrong—winning or losing. Pointing to the correct bowl even when there is only one bowl from which to choose will seem like a great accomplishment to your one-year-old.

Finale

Try playing the same hide-the-ball game with three identical bowls instead of two. Adding another hiding place will make the game more challenging. At first, just let your toddler watch as you put the ball under one of the bowls. Wait a few seconds, then ask him to point to the bowl that covers the ball. When using more than two places to hide the ball, just remembering where it is will be a challenge.

Encore

Play a guessing game with a marshmallow, a cookie, a cracker, or other treat. Place it in one hand. Then put your hands behind your back and ask your toddler to pick which hand has the treat. Putting your hands behind your back will confuse him at first.

           © Instructional Fair • TS Denison

Bubbles!

Borne, like thy bubbles, onward: from a boy. . . .
—Lord Byron

Overture..

Toddlers enjoy causing things to happen. For example, when blowing into a bubble wand they can make beautiful bubbles that will float through the air. For children this age, making bubbles is magical.

Performance..

Play: To teach your toddler how to blow bubbles, play with bubbles and bubble wands.
What you will need: Bottle of bubbles with wand
How to play: Pick a warm sunny day and go outside to blow bubbles. Show your toddler how to blow through the wand to make bubbles. You will have to hold the bottle of bubble soap and the wand, but your toddler will be able to blow the bubbles. If your toddler loves to blow bubbles and you want to make your own bubble soap, it is easy.
Directions: Mix one part dishwashing liquid with ten parts of water. Add a little less or little more water to create bubble soap that is easy to blow. To increase the bubble's surface tension, you can add glycerine, available at any pharmacy. To make interesting wands, bend a copper wire into a closed shape and attach to one end of a drinking straw, or use a berry basket, plastic rings for a six-pack of soda, and so on.

Finale.....................................

Bubbles can also be used in the bathtub where it will not matter if they are spilled. Add a drop of food coloring to the bubble soap. As long as there is enough light in the room to shine through the bubbles, you will see colorful bubbles.

Encore.....................................

A sink will provide an excellent spot for your toddler's play. Fill a sink half full of warm water. Then add detergent to the water to create mounds of bubbles. Provide a safe stool for your toddler to use while standing next to the sink. In the sink, place plastic measuring cups and serving spoons for scooping and pouring bubbles.

Sniff, Sniff

There was an old woman, and she sold puddings and pies.
Hot pies and cold pies to sell.
Wherever she goes you may follow her by the smell.
—Traditional Rhyme

Overture

From the moment a baby is born, aroma holds special experiences for him. Your toddler's special toys such as stuffed animals and dolls will have a certain scent. The familiar scent of his dolls and bears will be comforting and soothing to him. He may object when you wash a favorite blanket, because it will smell differently after going through the washer and dryer.

Performance

Play: To encourage your toddler to pick up things and smell them, play "Sniff, Sniff."
What you will need: Citrus fruits (lemon, orange, tangerine, lime), four plastic bowls, knife
How to play: Show your toddler the four fruits. Roll them. Sniff them. Feel them. Then using the knife, cut off the peels. Cut each peel into little pieces and place them in individual bowls. Hold up each bowl one at a time and tell your toddler, "Sniff, sniff." Say the name of the fruit as your toddler is inhaling the aroma of the peels. When finished, let your toddler eat small pieces of the fruit.

Finale

Play sniffing games. Choose three familiar foods like cheese, chocolate, and lemons. Place all three foods on the table in front of your toddler. Have him close his eyes. Then hold one of the foods up to his nostrils and tell him to "Sniff, sniff." Then place the food back on the table. When he opens his eyes, have him smell all three again and try to point to the one he thinks he was smelling. On other occasions, play with a variety of different foods.

Encore

As your toddler becomes aware of aromas, provide a lot of aromatic experiences including:
- ◆ Visit a bakery while donuts are being made. Smell and taste a warm donut.
- ◆ Visit a rose garden. Show the toddler how to sniff the aroma of flowers.
- ◆ Visit a perfume counter at a department store. Let your child sniff some perfume samples.
- ◆ Visit a barn where hay is stored. Enjoy the aroma of fresh hay.
- ◆ If no one in your family is allergic to cut grass, take a walk in the grass after it has been mowed. Rest in it. Show your toddler how to sniff the freshly mowed grass.
- ◆ While cooking in the kitchen, have your toddler sniff the aroma of coffee perking, chocolate chip cookies baking, cabbage boiling, etc.
- ◆ Visit a specialty store that sells aromatic creams and lotions. Rub sample lotions on your toddler's hands and encourage him to sniff.

© Instructional Fair • TS Denison

Keeping Track

Milestone	Date	Comments
Can imitate many actions		
Can combine objects in play		
Can use trial-and-error to discover solutions		
Can retrieve a hidden toy		
Can hide a toy for another to find		
Can look up and down on command		
Can scribble with a crayon		
Can imitate sounds: cough, sneeze, and so on		
Understands accomplish-ments and likes praise		
Can play independently for periods of time		
Can search for another person in the house		
Understands "push," "pull," and "lift"		
Can find things hidden out of sight		
Will learn how to blow bubbles		
Will pick up things to smell them		

"Mine!"

Social/Emotional Development

 ### Contemplate

One-year-olds are relatively compliant. They go where they are taken and are usually happy to explore the world by picking up and manipulating objects. But by the end of the next six months, your toddler will have a mind of his own. His newfound mobility, crawling and walking, will enable him to explore his environment more fully.

When you tell a one-year-old "No," it is still easy to distract him, However, by the time he is one-and-a-half, he will be much less distractible. He will know what he wants and he will do the things he knows how to do to get what he wants—cry, scream, kick, yell, and throw things. Yes, sometime during this period you will no doubt see your toddler throw a tantrum. See the tips for dealing with tantrums on the next page.

Social/Emotional Milestones: Twelve to Eighteen Months

◆ May demonstrate anger by throwing things
◆ May strike out at a parent in anger
◆ Will enjoy roughhousing with Father or siblings
◆ Will show affection for stuffed toys and dolls by hugging
◆ Will demonstrate rhythm by dancing and moving to music
◆ Will love to have an audience
◆ May offer a toy to another child when told to do so
◆ May be afraid of the dark
◆ May not like being left by his caregiver
◆ May begin to cooperate when being dressed
◆ May have ambiguous feelings about growing independence
◆ Will begin to feel self-pride

© Instructional Fair • TS Denison

 General Tips

Temper tantrums are a toddler's way of releasing pent-up tension. When your toddler gets worked up and loses control, remember, she is not thinking straight. There is no way she can figure out how to get back on track by herself. When she gets angry and frustrated, she will need an adult to do all the right things to calm her. What are the right things? Each child is unique, and what calms one may not calm another. On different occasions try each of the following to see which method works best with your toddler:

Validate her feelings—Tell her you understand that she is angry (hungry, tired, sick, overly excited). Explain that all people get angry (hungry, tired, sick, overly excited) and you feel like that sometimes, too. Then calmly state your plan to help her feel less angry (hungry, tired, sick, overly excited). Say something like this: "I know you are tired of shopping. I am going to take you home as soon as I pay for the groceries so you can have a nap." If your child is on the floor of the store kicking and crying, just stay with her and let her finish her tantrum. Ignore those around you who tell you to spank her or think they know how to handle the situation. Chances are, they have not dealt with a toddler in many, many years.

Switch gears—Do something else. For example: if your toddler is throwing a tantrum because she cannot get out of the shopping cart at the supermarket, you might say something like this: "I am going to take you out of the cart and hold you for a minute. We will look at these apples together. Then I will put you back in the cart just long enough to pay for the food. When we get to the car, I will take you out of the cart again and we will go home."

Distract her—Suggest that she breathe deeply. Demonstrate deep breathing. Get close to her and begin a deep breathing routine. If she does not join in and become calmer, at least *you* will feel calmer.

Hold her in your arms—If your child is not kicking and swinging her arms, pick her up and hold her. Swaddling is not only for infants. Being held tightly gives toddlers a feeling of security that they especially need when they are out of control.

Listen to her crying—Do not try to stop her tears. Sit quietly by her side and just listen to her. Do not say a word. Make eye contact, and let your silence tell her "I know you are very angry." Just acknowledging her anger will let her know that you care about her feelings.

Demonstrate calmness—Do not overreact to her anger. If you are in a public place and people are staring at your screaming, kicking child, you may want to silence her at any price. Do not let onlookers pressure you into doing something that is not your style. Smile at them. Smile at your toddler. Wait. Her anger will soon be spent and she will need a calm adult there to greet her when she settles down.

Get silly—Sing a song, make faces, or in some way find a bit of humor in the situation. Teaching your child to laugh at herself once in a while will give her something to fall back on later in life.

No matter what method you use, just keep in mind that crying is the only voice your toddler has when dealing with all her emotions. Try to imagine what it would be like to spend years without being able to tell people what you want.

Ping-Pong Pitch

Billy, Billy, come and play,
While the sun shines bright as day.
—Traditional Rhyme

Overture

Watch your toddler when he is angry, and you may see him throw, kick, or bang his toys. Although throwing things is unsafe, it may seem to him to be the only means he has to control things. He may need to release tension; therefore, tossing the first thing he can get his hands on will make sense to him. Allowing him to throw things when he is not angry will diffuse the importance of throwing as an act of anger.

Performance

Play: To help your toddler demonstrate anger in appropriate ways, give him plenty of opportunities to throw things when he is not angry.
What you will need: Several tennis balls (or table tennis balls), blanket
How to play: Lay out a blanket. Have your toddler try to pitch the balls onto the blanket. Show him how to retrieve the balls and toss them again. See how hard he can toss them. Challenge him by moving the blanket a bit farther away. Also try throwing other safe things at a target hung on a wall or blanket placed on the ground, including dry leaves, marshmallows, tennis balls, paper wads, or paper airplanes.

Finale

During a tantrum is not a good time to teach your toddler anything. No one can listen when he is angry. However, on another occasion when your toddler is not angry, talk to him about feelings. Show him how to deal with his anger in a number of appropriate ways:
- Pounding on clay with a wooden mallet
- Ripping up newspapers into confetti
- Stomping feet in a mad-as-I-can-get dance
- Clapping hands in a loud-as-I-can-make-it clap
- Going to a place where echoes can be heard and screaming
- Stomping in a puddle

Encore

Dealing with anger in appropriate ways is not a skill a toddler can comprehend. However, you can do much to manage your child's anger. You can give him activities to help relieve tension before it boils over. You can present ways to handle stress in games and activities that will be fun for him. The most important thing you will teach your child about anger will not come from anything you say or games you play. Basically he will learn how to handle anger by watching you when you are stressed out. If you accept anger as a part of the human condition and you manage it appropriately, you will be sending your toddler an important message about negative feelings—"We all have them; having feelings is part of the human experience."

© Instructional Fair • TS Denison

Soothing Baby

Billy, Billy, come along,
And I will sing a pretty song.
—Traditional Rhyme

Overture

When toddlers get very angry, sometimes they will strike out at parents but they hardly ever strike out at others. How you respond to your toddler's anger will send her a clear message about dealing with anger. Acknowledge her anger and tell her hitting is inappropriate.

Performance

Play: Give your toddler an opportunity to relax and release tension by giving her massages.
What you will need: Lotion
How to play: Lay a blanket on the floor in front of you. Place the toddler on her back on the blanket. Put a little lotion on her feet and gently massage each foot for 30 seconds. Then massage both ankles and the lower part of each leg for 30 seconds. Continue moving up her body, massaging each area for 30 seconds including:

◆ Knees and thighs
◆ Stomach and chest
◆ Shoulders and upper arms
◆ Elbows and lower arms
◆ Hand and fingers
◆ Neck and face

Roll the toddler over onto her stomach and finish by massaging her head and back.

Finale

When you see your toddler is full of anxiety, fear, or sadness, use a mini-massage on her chest near her heart to help soothe her. Other ways to help your toddler relax include taking her for long walks, playing soft music, and rocking her in your lap while singing a lullaby.

Encore

Verbally acknowledging your toddler's anger will help defuse some of it. You may want to say something like this: "I know you are angry because you cannot have cookies right now. Nevertheless, you have to eat your lunch soon and you may not have the cookies." When you verbalize that you know why she is angry, the frustration of trying to tell you what she wants will go away. She will know that you do know what she wants and you are not going to give it to her. Then instead of dealing with frustration, she will only have to deal with her disappointment.

Social/Emotional Development Twelve- to Eighteen-Month-Old

Bear Wrestling

I am a Bear of Very Little Brain,
and long words Bother me.
—*"Pooh Bear"*
by Alan Alexander Milne

Overture

Watch your toddler and you will often see him testing his own strength. He will lift and carry heavy objects to prove his own power. It makes a toddler feel good to know he has a powerful body.

Performance

Play: To fill your toddler's roughhousing needs, play "Bear Wrestling."
What you will need: Well padded floor—a thick carpet or padded quilt, or grassy area
How to play: Put your toddler on the floor or grass beside you. Get down on all fours and growl like a bear. Grrrrr, grrrrr—without taking your "paws" off the ground go after the toddler. Use your head to gently nudge him. Let him set the pace of the game. Grrrr, grrrrr—try to crawl on top of him. After a while, try to crawl away from him. To end the game, roll over on your back and surrender to the "baby bear."

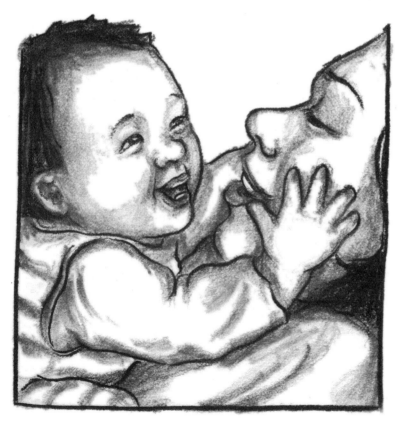

Finale

Another good roughhousing game is to lie on your back and let your toddler crawl or walk over you. Say something like, "Come on tough stuff; come and wrestle with me." Roll and curl up in a ball. Use your hands to try to get your toddler to slow down his "attack." Hold him tightly, sometimes, so he cannot get free for a second. Again, let your child set the pace of the game. Play in such a way that your toddler feels like he is powerful.

Encore

Encourage the toddler's siblings, uncles, or aunts to wrestle with him, too. He will enjoy the pace set by different wrestling opponents. Wrestling is a good game if you want to wear him out before going to bed at night. The physical contact in wrestling will ground your toddler and allow him to celebrate his own growing strength.

© Instructional Fair • TS Denison

Good Night, Bear

Be always like the lamb so mild,
A kind, and sweet, and gentle child.
Sleep, baby, sleep.
　　　　　　　　—Traditional Rhyme

Overture

Resistance to going to sleep at night often begins in toddlerhood. By nighttime most toddlers are overstimulated and overtired. Usually the whole family is home and exciting things are happening. Going to bed separates the toddler from the family and the excitement, so it is no wonder that toddlers hate going to bed.

Performance

Play: To help ease the sadness of bedtime and at the same time encourage your toddler to show affection for stuffed toys and dolls, play "Good Night, Bear."

What you will need: No special equipment is needed to play this game.

How to play: When it is time for your toddler to go to bed, carry her into the bedroom. Go around the room hugging or kissing and telling the toys and objects in the room "Good night." If she can name the objects, your toddler can say the greeting, too. If she cannot name the objects, she can just say "Good night" and wave good-bye. Examples:

◆ Good night, closet. (*Close door.*)
◆ Good night, bear. (*Tuck bear in bed.*)
◆ Good night, wagon. (*Push against the wall.*)

The last thing you might say "Good night" to is the light, as you switch it off. Tuck your toddler into bed and tell her, "Good night. I love you best of all."

Finale

If after saying "Good night" to toys and objects your toddler still needs to wind, try rocking her, telling her a story, singing her a lullaby, or giving her a back rub. The important thing will be consistency. Remember, a bedtime ritual should not change. It is something that your toddler can depend upon every night. It is these rituals that your toddler will expect for her security.

Encore

If your toddler is the active type, it may take her half an hour or more to unwind. Having that time to be with her every night is very important. When your schedule will not allow you to fulfill the nightly ritual, do not be surprised if your toddler has difficulty going to sleep. Leaving some soothing music playing in her room at night to help her to relax and fall asleep.

Social/Emotional Development **Twelve- to Eighteen-Month-Old**

Butterfly Flittering

There, little baby, there you go.
Up to the ceiling, down to the ground,
Backwards and forwards, round and round.
—Traditional Rhyme

Overture

Watch how your toddler moves to music, and you will see how natural rhythm is for children. They do not have to be taught to keep a beat; it will come from within.

Performance

Play: To encourage your toddler to enjoy music, listen to recorded music and play "Butterfly Flittering."

What you will need: Four colorful silk scarves, classical or jazz music

How to play: Pin or tie a silk scarf to each of your toddler's wrists. Do the same for yourself. Play music and demonstrate how to move in a free way. Your toddler may only want to stand and move his arms to the music, or he may move around flapping his arms like a butterfly flittering. Play slow, relaxing music.

Finale

Use movement games as winding-down activities before naps. Play the games sitting in bed and moving the upper part of the body to very, very slow music. Have your child close his eyes and slowly move his arms as if drifting:

- Like a snowflake falling to the ground
- Like a feather floating in the air
- Like a tree moving in a breeze
- Like a star twinkling in the sky
- Like a hawk soaring in the sky
- Like a snowman melting in the sunshine
- Like a cake baking in an oven
- Like leaves falling from a tree

Encore

Provide a wide range of imaginary situations for your toddler to play. Stimulating the possibilities for fantasy play will enrich his ability to make up his own ideas for pretend play.

© Instructional Fair • TS Denison

Take a Bow

Dance little baby, and mother will sing,
With the merry carol, ding, ding, ding!
—Traditional Rhyme

Overture

Watch, and you will see your toddler's emotional growth. Emerging will be her new sense of independence and social power expressed in her self-pride. One of the first things your toddler will say when she learns to talk is "Watch me." She will love being the center of attention.

Performance

Play: Toddlers love to have an audience. To provide your toddler with time where she can be in the spotlight, play "Take a Bow."

What you will need: Any well-lit spot that can become your toddler's stage

How to play: Show your toddler the "stage." Sit where you can watch her dance. Play music. If your toddler dances and moves on her own, enjoy the show. If she does not understand that she is the main performance, demonstrate by dancing and moving to the music on the "stage." Then tell her you want to watch her dance. You might act as an emcee and introduce her performance. "Ladies and gentlemen, boys and girls, introducing Baby (toddler's name), the world famous ballerina." Most toddlers will dance as long as someone is watching. Applaud often for your toddler. Invite family members to watch, too. When her performance has ended, tell her, "Take a bow." You may have to teach her how to take a bow. Applaud loudly for her. Giving your toddler five or ten minutes every evening to perform for you will do much to advance her positive self-esteem.

Finale

Use the "stage" to have your child do things besides dance. If she learns to turn a somersault, invite the whole family to sit and watch her perform her new feat. When she learns to hop, or skip, or twirl around, make it a special occasion. Celebrate her every accomplishment and let her know how special she is by arranging formal presentations to others on the "stage." Always end the performances by telling her, "Take a bow."

Encore

As your toddler begins to grasp that she is a distinct individual, she will be more and more motivated to prove herself. When she "shows off" for others, it is her way of asking for approval. Lavish your toddler with praise and appreciation for her accomplishments so she can grow to be filled with self-worth. Encourage her performances by:

- Having props or costumes
- Painting her face
- Taking photographs and making videos
- Having curtains or backdrops for the performances

Social/Emotional Development Twelve- to Eighteen-Month-Old

Playmates

Punch and Judy fought for a pie,
Punch gave Judy a knock in the eye.
—Traditional Rhyme

Overture

Watch your child as he is getting closer to one-and-a-half years old, and you may see that he will offer a toy to another child when told to do so. He might not want to share, but at this stage of development, toddlers usually do as they are told, especially in the presence of others.

Performance

Play: To encourage your toddler to offer a toy to another child when told to do so, arrange for your toddler to play with another toddler.

What you will need: Toys, supervised place to play

How to play: Arranging for your toddler to play with another toddler for half an hour each week will provide him with a valuable opportunity to learn from a peer. Because you cannot predict a toddler's behavior, the pair should be supervised at all times. If either toddler hits or attacks the other, separate them. Explain gently that the other child has feelings and does not like to be hurt. Physically or aggressively disciplining a toddler will reinforce this negative behavior. Gently explain to your toddler that the other child will not want to come back to play if she is afraid; this will usually be enough to stop the behavior.

Finale

Take your toddler to places where other children play, such as parks and playgrounds. He will enjoy watching the way older toddlers and preschoolers do things. Your toddler will learn more from watching other children than he can ever learn at home by himself. His social development depends upon time spent with other children.

Encore

Toddlers play alongside each other but they rarely interact or cooperate. Each will be caught up in his own play. They may imitate each other, but toddlers at this age are too young to interact with each other.

© Instructional Fair • TS Denison

Lights Out!

Teddy Bear, Teddy Bear, turn out the lights.
Teddy Bear, Teddy Bear, say good night.
—Jump Rope Rhyme

Overture

Watch and determine if your toddler is afraid of the dark. Now that she is beginning to have an imagination, she may think monsters live under her bed, a bear is in her closet, or have some other frightening thoughts that emerge when the lights go out. When she expresses fear of the dark, honor her fear and find ways to reassure her.

Performance

Play: To help your toddler not be afraid of the dark, play "Lights Out!"
What you will need: Flashlight
How to play: Seat your toddler safely on the floor in a room that can be darkened (or play the game at night). Tell your toddler you are going to play a game in the dark. Turn out the lights. Turn on the flashlight. Let her hold the flashlight and play with it. Look at familiar objects in the room with the light from the flashlight. Talk about the objects. Use the flashlight to make shadows on the walls.

Finale

Things you can do to comfort a toddler who wakes up in the middle of the night include:
- ◆ Leave a night-light glowing.
- ◆ Give her a flashlight to use in the middle of the night if she wants.
- ◆ Go into your child's room and comfort her; rock her back to sleep.
- ◆ Sit beside the bed, reach in and comfort her but do not pick her up.
- ◆ Sit in a chair in your child's room and talk to her but do not touch her or take her out of the bed.
- ◆ Turn on some low, soft music that will soothe her and then leave the room, closing the door.
- ◆ Put a soft, stuffed animal in bed with her and tell her to go to sleep, then leave the room.

Encore

Nightmares sometimes awaken toddlers. Some toddlers cry out in fright or anger while they are sleeping. How you handle middle-of-the-night awakenings will be up to you. Some parents rush to the child and cuddle and hold her to make her feel secure. Other parents believe that going into the child's room will reinforce the nighttime needing of comfort so they let their toddler cry until she falls back to sleep. The important thing is to be consistent. If sometimes someone comes when she cries and sometimes they do not, the child will be confused. She will think crying might bring someone, so she will tend to cry longer.

Peekaboo, Baby!

Peekaboo, Baby, I see you.
Peekaboo, Baby, you see me, too.

Overture

Watch your toddler when you have to leave him. He may feel anxious when left with a baby-sitter or someone other than his regular caregiver. He may even cry when you leave the room. Separation, in various degrees, is a problem with many toddlers.

Performance

Play: To teach your toddler that people leave and then come back, play "Peekaboo, Baby!"
What you will need: No special equipment is needed to play this game.
How to play: Place your child on the floor in a room. Tell him you are going to play a game. Leave the room. As you go, tell your toddler you will be right back. Wait two or three seconds outside the door, and then pop your head back in and say, "Peekaboo, Baby!" Go up to your toddler and give him a kiss or hug or show affection in a familiar way. Then tell your child you are going to leave again. This time stay in the hall out of sight for five or ten seconds. Then again pop back into the room while saying, "Peekaboo, Baby!" Repeat, staying out of sight for varied amounts of time.

Finale

This game can be played with a silly hat as a prop. When you put on a particular hat (worn during the playing of the game), tell your toddler you are going to play "Peekaboo, Baby!" Then whenever he sees you putting on the hat and leaving the room, he knows you are playing a game. Next, let him wear the hat and leave the room. He will soon learn to say "Peekaboo" as he pops back into the room.

Encore

There are ways to make your departure less traumatic for your toddler including:

- ◆ Take time to say good-bye in a cheerful, non-hurried way.
- ◆ Give him a concrete term for when you will be back.
- ◆ Tell him something you will do together when you get back.
- ◆ Embrace and show affection, and as you are leaving wave good-bye, throw him a kiss, or in some other way demonstrate a signal of love.

© Instructional Fair • TS Denison

Where Does This Go?

Darby and Joan were dressed in black,
Buttons and buckles behind their back.
Foot for foot, and knee for knee,
Turn about Darby's company.
—Traditional Rhyme

Overture

Watch your toddler as you are dressing her, and you will be able to tell if looking nice is important to her or not. For some toddlers getting dressed is a bother. Some toddlers hate to have their hair brushed or their faces and hands washed. Sometimes, complimenting your toddler will make her more willing to cooperate when getting dressed and presentable. "We are going to make you look beautiful again today."

Performance

Play: To teach your toddler to cooperate with you when you are getting her dressed, play "Where Does This Go?"

What you will need: Clothes to put on your toddler including shoes and socks

How to play: As you are dressing your toddler, hold up a piece of clothing and ask, "Where does this go?" Ask silly questions about the clothes. Your toddler may be so amused by the game that she will want to cooperate and help you out. Examples:

◆ Do I put these socks on your ears? (*Try putting the socks on her ears.*)
◆ Not on your ears? Then where do I put these? (*Wait for your toddler to help you by indicating where to put the socks.*)
◆ Do I put these shoes on your elbows? (*Try putting them on her elbows.*)
◆ Where does this shirt go? On your legs? (*Try putting the shirt on her legs.*)

Finale

On other occasions, sing a little song while you are dressing or brushing her hair. Use the familiar tune "Here We Go 'Round the Mulberry Bush" to sing a dressing song:

This is the way we change (toddler's name) diaper, change (toddler's name) diaper, change (toddler's name) diaper,
This is the way we change (toddler's name) diaper, early in the morning.
This is the way we put on (toddler's name) shirt, put on (toddler's name) shirt, put on (toddler's name) shirt.
This is the way we put on (toddler's name) shirt, early in the morning.

Encore

Here is a game you can play to encourage your toddler to cooperate when you are brushing her hair. Have her hold a hand mirror and say, "Make sure I am doing this right." Tell your toddler to use the mirror to watch as you are brushing her hair. You can do the same thing when brushing her teeth. Using a hand mirror to see what is happening makes the process more interesting for your toddler and lets her participate in it.

We Love You

Roses are red, violets are blue,
I love you, they do, too.

Overture

The most important things you can communicate to your child are love, a sense of belonging to a family, and positive self-esteem. Toddlers are caught up in a complex web of ambiguous feelings. They want to be independent at times, but at the same time, they want never to be left alone. They want to grow, but they do not want to give up the benefits of being a baby. They want to get all of the attention and not share that attention with siblings, but they like belonging to a family.

Performance

Play: To promote your toddler's feelings of belonging, play "We Love You."
What you will need: All the family members
How to play: At a mealtime or other family gathering, have each member of the family tell what they love most about every other family member. Begin with what everyone loves about your toddler. Write down what the family members say they love about your toddler. Later read the list to him again and again.

Finale

Telling your toddler that you love him, each and every day, is important to his emotional well-being. Play a game of "I Love Your (name a body part)." Touch each part of your toddler's face and body and say, "I love your (name the part)" and say something it does. Examples:
- ◆ I love your nose; it helps you smell the roses.
- ◆ I love your legs; they make you run fast.
- ◆ I love your eyes; through them you can see me smiling at you.
- ◆ I love your hands; they can scribble beautiful lines.

Encore

Toddlers wants to belong to the family but do not really know how. Teach your toddler that you all belong together with activities such as:
- ◆ Good night kisses from every member
- ◆ Smiling whenever your eyes meet
- ◆ Greeting those who enter the room
- ◆ Eating meals together as often as possible
- ◆ Taking days off to be together
- ◆ Going on family outings
- ◆ Talking as a group at least once a day

© Instructional Fair • TS Denison

Look at Me!

Look at me, what do you see.
Look at me, smart as can be.

Overture

People form their life-long feelings about their self-worth when they are children. Your toddler is deciding her importance based on how you treat her. Celebrating your toddler's abilities will build her positive self-esteem.

Performance

Play: To encourage your toddler to celebrate her own growth and learning, create a "Look at Me!" photograph album.

What you will need: Camera and film

How to play: This project may take several days or a week of photographing, but the creation will be well worth the effort and time. It might be fun to dress your toddler in a variety of costumes. As you take photographs, have your toddler demonstrate some of the things she has learned this year including:

- Rolling over
- Sitting up
- Standing without support
- Walking
- Playing with a busy box
- Filling and emptying containers
- Grasping two blocks with one hand
- Turning pages of a book
- Pointing
- Holding a large ball
- Climbing stairs on hands and knees
- Sliding down stairs on stomach

- Opening a hinged box
- Sniffing something
- Playing in a sandbox
- Playing in a tub of water
- Looking up
- Looking down
- Scribbling
- Pushing something
- Pulling something
- Lifting something
- Blowing bubbles
- Waving good-bye

Finale

When the film is developed, put one photograph on each page of a notebook or scrapbook. Use a broad-tipped black marker to write one word or phrase under each photograph (see above). When you finish the book, look at it often and read the words to your toddler. With great fanfare, bring out the book when company comes to your house. Share it with her peers. Cherish her today, and someday she will remember her childhood as a great treasure.

Encore

Start a collection of your toddler's drawings and scribblings. Keep a scrapbook or glue everything collage-fashion to a large poster board. Display the work where family and visitors can see it. Treasuring your toddler's work and praising her accomplishments will build her ego and help her develop positive self-esteem.

Keeping Track

Milestone	Date	Comments
Might throw things to demonstrate anger		
Might strike out at parents when angry		
Can roughhouse with larger people		
Can show affection for stuffed toys		
Can move with rhythm to music		
Will enjoy "showing off" for an audience		
May offer a toy to another child		
May be afraid of the dark		
May object to being left by a caregiver		
May cooperate while being dressed		
May begin to feel independent		
Will begin to feel he/she belongs to the family		
Will begin to feel proud of accomplishments		

DISCARDED from New Hanover County Public Library

© Instructional Fair • TS Denison